THE BROKEN ROAD

JOEL 2:25

MARY BOYLE

ISBN 979-8-88751-122-1 (paperback)
ISBN 979-8-88751-123-8 (digital)

Christian Faith Publishing
832 Park Avenue
Meadville, PA 16335
www.christianfaithpublishing.com

Printed in the United States of America

ACKNOWLEDGMENTS

I HAVE MANY acknowledgments, and I may miss a few but not on purpose. I want to thank, praise, and acknowledge my Lord and Savior, Jesus Christ, who without His protection I would not be writing this today. I want to thank my husband, Mike, who has encouraged me through many periods of growth and writing. I want to acknowledge my friends Nancy, Julie, Frances, LaSydia, Dotti, and many, many more for their prayers and encouragement. I need to acknowledge several artists and authors for the contributions to my life through their music and/or writings: Beth Moore, Zach Williams, Travis Cottrell, and Selah.

I have written a lot of papers and thesis on many, many topics. To this date, this was the hardest thing I have ever written because it reached deep into my soul, and I hurt all over again. I have come to understand Paul and his teachings about the flesh and how we deal with it every day. The battle rages, on but the war has already been won through Jesus. My heart has hurt as I finished this manuscript. Things that are very private and special that only the Lord and I need to know have risen to the surface of my mind to add to my broken heart. Someone once said, "It is not the truth we know but the truth we obey that makes the difference in our lives." God heals and restores the brokenhearted. I rest in Him, for He is my rock and redeemer.

INTRODUCTION

THE BROKEN ROAD has been a long journey home to the Father in heaven. Even though the road has taken many, many detours, the road has always led me back to my Father in heaven through Jesus Christ His Son. My journey has not been an unusual story; however, several friends have suggested that it's worthy of paper and pen. As I try to write and re-create many of the circumstances within my life, I want to make it known that I do not place blame to any one person, nor do I hold any grudge toward anyone mentioned in my story. My story does not try to cause harm to those mentioned, only a sharing of my life. I pray that my story, with the help of Christ Jesus, will help someone else to understand that we are not alone in our day-to-day battles of life. With the help of the Holy Spirit and God's hand, I pray you, the reader, feel the healing power of Jehovah Rapha, the God that heals.

CHAPTER 1

Train up a child in the way he should go, and
when he is old, he will not depart from it.

—Proverbs 22:6

Train up a child in the way he should go… The Lord instructs us to train up our children. After all, they are precious gifts from God. In my early years, I was raised in a family that attended and was active in the Methodist Church. Methodists are fine, God-fearing people just like the Baptists (which I became later in life). My parents set out to raise my sister, brother, and me as best as they could. They were hardworking, honest Christians that had very horrible childhoods. My parents loved each other very deeply, but the emotional demons from their pasts interfered and undermined their efforts to be good examples for their children. As I look back on my life, I don't remember a time when there was no underlying conflict in my life.

When I was three, we moved to a little house in College Park, Georgia. I remember it had the tiniest kitchen. When everyone sat at the kitchen table, our chairs backed up to the walls and stove. My dad added on a large room to the back of the house to give us more room. My cousins lived several blocks down the street and up a hill. This was one of the many suburbs built in the 1950s during the expansion era after World War II. All the neighboring houses were similar to the one we lived in. It was at this house that I experienced my first memory of domestic unrest within our family.

One night at dinner, my parents were arguing loudly, saying unkind words to one another, when my father decided to leave. This was his nature, to leave in the middle of arguments. My father was not one to face conflict head on. Like I mentioned, our kitchen was very tiny, and my chair backed up to the stove. When my dad went to cross between my chair and the stove to leave, he accidently turned over a pot of hot vegetable oil on me. The memory I have is sitting in a hospital room screaming and crying from the pain of the burns. Miraculously, I do not have any physical scars from the incident, but it was the beginning of a long trail of verbal abuse within our family.

I am not writing a book about how bad my parents were while raising me; however, my inner perceptions began to grow, and I felt like I was unloved and unworthy all my life. When I was five, we moved to another area of College Park where there was more yard and open spaces. My sister was three, and my brother was one. The elementary school we attended was less than a half of a mile from our house. I attended Cliftondale Elementary School from first through seventh grades. There were not a lot of other children around to play with. Our mother worked in downtown Atlanta, and our father worked for the State and went to school at night until the end of 1963, when he graduated from law school.

I know in my heart we had to have had some good times, but I don't really remember many at all. All I remember is not ever being *good* enough in school, in dress, in appearance. My own grandmothers on my mother's side complained openly about me when I visited them. I bit my nails as a child, and these grandmothers had a field day with that, comparing me with second cousins who evidently were favored over us. As I got older, I began to change, as most young girls do. I gained some weight and was heavier than my sister and the other ideal cousins. As soon as I would enter this grandmother's house, she would take me straight to the bathroom and weigh me to see if I had gained more weight. This process began when I was about ten and continued until I was about sixteen when I refused to visit her anymore.

Another annoying thing I remember was when I would get the croup (every winter), they would make me eat Vick's VapoRub, which I would promptly throw up. This would make them mad at me, but I would get sick from their home remedies. I hated going to their house, as I could not please either one of them.

When I look back over my life and my perspective of how my own mother was treated by her mother and grandmother, I realize that they were probably the main causes of my mother's own problems and feelings of insecurities. If these grandmothers treated us the way they did, I cannot imagine what life was like as a child for my mother. My mother was born on July 29, 1932 during the Great Depression. She was named Elizabeth. No middle name, simply Elizabeth. Later, her brother, William (Bill) Clarence was born March 10, 1934. It was that year, 1934, that my mother's father died from a logging accident. This left my grandmother with two young children. She promptly moved back in with her mother and eleven other siblings.

This was not an ideal place to bring up my mother and uncle, as all the siblings were boys. I heard through the rumor mill that my mother may have been abused as a young teenager. I cannot confirm any of the stories surrounding my mother because she never spoke about them to me. Most family members never spoke about anyone's problems within the family. Most of the serious problems were hidden in a closet. As I mentioned, my mother's problems began a long time before she and my father ever met.

My father's family was a working-class family from south Atlanta, just like my mother's family. My father was born January 30, 1929, the same year as the stock market crashed that triggered the Great Depression. My grandfather was an electrician for the railroad and was being called back to work when he had an automobile accident and lost his left arm. This was in 1930 when my father was a year old. My father's family lost their home, profession, and arm within about thirty days. My grandfather and grandmother Bryant, with my father, moved in with her parents. Life was hard during the Depression, but my father remembers most people looking out for each other.

My grandmother Bryant went to work at various retail jobs in Atlanta. My grandfather could only pick up odd jobs due to his disability. My grandfather drank alcohol and was verbally abusive. My father does not talk about his childhood much because of the embarrassing, unstable homelife. My father was raised to feel and be a *victim*. He is still angered and hurt when those memories are stirred up.

These parents of mine, Weyman and Elizabeth, met, fell in love, and married. They tried hard to have a family that was not characterized by their own previous experiences. They married in 1950, the year my dad came home from the Korean War. He was stationed in Japan during the war, and he never saw combat. He had many friends, however, that did experience the war, and my dad was always grateful he did not have to fight.

So now we are back to where I come in, born in September of 1954. The first grandchild on both sides of the family; however, I cannot say I was spoiled, though others will disagree. I have many photos from my childhood, and in each one it appears that I was a very happy and loved child. As I grew up, I could not get past the ugly feelings that I was not loved. Still to this day, as I write, those feelings creep up and haunt me. Those feelings were real to me then and now. Today, I know from my father that I was truly loved, even though I personally did not *feel* loved. More than ever I miss my mother and wish I could have known her as an adult. Maybe I could have worked through these *feelings* or maybe *lies* that I have believed for so long. I just don't really remember feeling good about anything I did.

Satan is clever, handsome, and deceiving. In 1 Peter 5:8, God's Word says, "Be sober, be vigilant; because your adversary the devil walks about like a roaring lion, seeking whom he may devour." As a child without clear understanding and guidance, I was fodder for Satan. I crossed paths with a lot of people, and most don't remember their early childhood. Oh how I wish I could erase some of my memories, those bad decisions and mistakes. I ask myself why God allows those memories to haunt me.

I was about four to five years old. I started school at age five, I turned six in September, and so I could start early. I remember we had a Black maid who took care of my brother and sister (they were younger) because my mother worked in Atlanta. My father worked in town for the Department of Corrections and went to school at night. He graduated when I was in third grade from John Marshall Law School.

I was always compared to my sister who was very good in school. The one time I finally made an *A* on my report card because I wanted the dollar too, it was in reading. My mother told me I would not get the reward because I should know how to read. After that, I never even tried to do much more than to pass my subjects because I could not compete with my sister's grades. I always wanted to be a part of the band at school. My mother would not let me because my grades were not where she thought they should be. My sister was able to join the band in third grade. I finally was able to join in sixth grade. I did not stay with the band after seventh grade because playing a string instrument in 1967 to 1968 was not "cool."

The only birthday party I ever remember being able to invite friends to was in the seventh grade. Not one person came except for cousins. I was devastated. I had never had a party where I could invite friends. I had been to other parties for friends from school and church, but I had never had one myself. I remember coming to the knowledge that it was true I was not liked nor loved by anyone. I could not figure out how to please everyone, so I could have the *feeling* of being loved. I was twelve, and I was already a failure. Where was my life heading?

At this point, looking back, I realize God has a plan. In Jeremiah 29:11, He tells us that "His ways are not our ways, and His thoughts are not our thoughts." When I was twelve, I went to a Valentine's banquet with a friend from the local Baptist church. I remember hearing something I had never heard before. God loved me, and He had a plan for me. I rushed down the aisle to have what the others had, Jesus. I was *saved* that night. I couldn't wait to get home and tell my mother.

She was not pleased with my news. I was not allowed to go to other church events with friends again. I was raised Methodist, and that was not very different from the Baptist, but my mother did not like it. But God still had a plan! In Psalm 27:10 He says, "When my

father and mother forsake me, then the LORD will take care of me."
What! I didn't know this!

One of God's promises is, He never leaves us nor forsakes us. At the tender age of twelve, I could not comprehend anything I could not physically see. I did not realize that on that Valentine's night that I had received Jesus the King of glory into my heart. He left the Holy Spirit within me to guide me and grow me spiritually. I did not grow, and I did not understand. My emotions were like a roller coaster, up and down, faster and faster, and getting nowhere fast. King David cried out to God in Psalm 3:3, "But You, O Lord, are a shield for and me, my glory and the One who lifts my head, I cried to the LORD with my voice, and he heard me from His holy hill."

CHAPTER 2

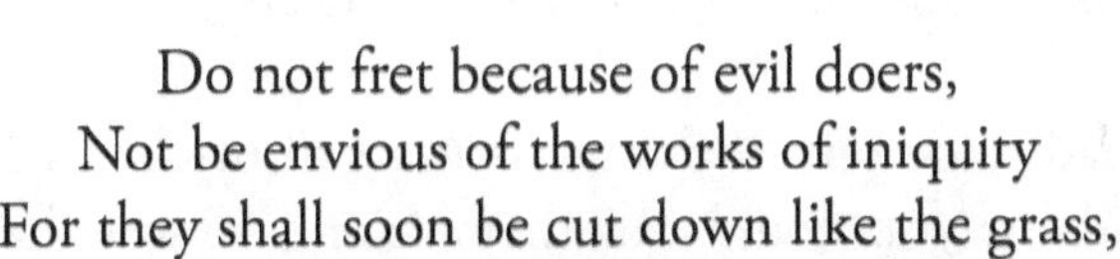

Do not fret because of evil doers,
Not be envious of the works of iniquity
For they shall soon be cut down like the grass,
And wither as the green herb.

—Psalm 37:1–2

WHEN EIGHTH GRADE started, I began to have new friends from the high school. These friends were not the best influences, and most of those friends from eighth grade dropped out by tenth grade to have children out of wedlock. However, they were my friends, and I now had a few who seemed to like me. At thirteen, my attitude toward both of my parents was not very good. I especially hated my mother because I had never felt loved nor had I ever been able to please her. My life at this point was being lived like a *victim* and was following the same pattern both of my parents' lives had followed. There is no victory in living as a *victim*. At thirteen, I thought I knew everything, and I was bucking the system every chance I got.

At this point of my life I was emulating everything I had been taught as a child. My parents fought with vicious, biting words and cursed each other in their anger. My father typically left during every fight. My mother took out her anger on us with a belt or a shoe. My whippings stopped when at thirteen, I was as strong as my mother, and I would not let go of the belt. I learned to use those same biting words to hurt my already tormented mother. Words like "I hate you" are something most children use but learn not to. I, however, meant every word I spoke because I had never felt anything different.

I remember talking to God one night when my parents were verbally fighting. I prayed that God would send me a husband that did not fuss and fight, one who would love me; I just was tired of all the screaming and yelling. Why was life like this? Were other families like ours? Even though I could not see or *feel* God working, He was protecting me because I had received His Son in my heart. God was walking with me down a very broken road.

Eighth grade Campbell High, Fairburn, Georgia

This had to be one of the worst years of my life. I had a handful of friends, if you could call them friends. I was hanging with the wrong people. I had very average grades, just enough to get by. Over spring break (April 14, Easter), my mother committed suicide. Needless to say I failed the last half of eighth grade. In James, the Bible tells us the tongue is a sharp sword. Words cannot be taken back once said, yet every day we use words to cut down, ridicule, complain, and destroy those around us.

My mother and father had an argument during Sunday dinner, and the whole family was in an uproar. My dad left. As usual during any conflict, my mother asked me if she took her life, would everyone be happy? I responded with "Sure, I hate you anyway."

Guess what? She locked herself in her bedroom and hung herself on the closet door. My sister begged me to try and get in the door. My brother was crying, and my sister was crying. I finally got an axe from the storage room, and my sister went outside to try and look in the window. The way she shouted "Momma," I axed through the door, and my sister was able to get her arm in and unlock the door. We pulled her down and laid her on the floor. My sister ran to get a neighbor. I tried to call for help. In 1968, we dialed the operator of the phone company for emergencies, and I talked so fast no one ever came. The two neighbors came and started CPR, and one neighbor called the police and asked for an ambulance. We lived in the lower end of College Park, and in 1968, the emergency ambulance came from the funeral home in Fairburn.

My mother was taken to Holy Family Hospital in Ben Hill. Someone finally found my dad. Neither parent came home that Sunday night. A relative showed up to spend the night. The next day, we went to the hospital to see our mother; it was our first experience with a hospital. She was connected to machines and looked like she was not there. It was my only chance to undo the words I had spoken the day before, yet she would not hear them. Later, we spent the night with my father's parents. It was there on Tuesday morning that my uncle came to tell us that my mother had died. How would I ever get over giving her permission to take her life because I said I hated her, and I did not care?

That afternoon, my aunt and uncle from North Carolina came to our house and helped to buy clothes or wash clothes and our hair, so we could be presentable at the funeral. The funeral was on Wednesday at Patterson's Funeral on Cascade Road. There were so many people there, and when we drove to the cemetery in McDonough, we took the expressway and for as far as I could see behind me, the cars kept coming. Funny that my mother never felt loved in her lifetime. Her childhood had been full of disappointment and abuse. She had passed on the same feelings to me. As an adult, I don't think she meant to, but she did not know how to stop the cycle of abuse. We do not know exactly why she took her life. I cannot judge her, I miss her, I love her, and I am very angry at her for leaving us.

Romans 8:28 says, "We know that all things work together for good for those who love God, who are called according to His purpose. For those whom He foreknew He also predestined to be conformed to the image of His Son, in order that He might be the first-born within a large family." I was thirteen the year my life crumbled the first time. My sister was eleven, and my brother was nine. We have all borne the marks of the victim, and the marks fade, but they do not go away this side of heaven. In Jeremiah 29:11 (NASB), it states, "For I know the plans that I have for you, declared the LORD, plans for welfare and not for calamity to give you a future and a hope." Lost, alone, unable to express myself, angry, angry at myself—how could I give her permission to harm herself? Remember Satan is clever; his demons took over my mother and destroyed her life. Satan also destroyed the rest of us too. My father, sister, and brother were all crushed by the weight of guilt and despair.

I forgot to mention that I was christened in the Methodist Church as a baby. My parents went to church every Sunday, and we were in Sunday school, vacation Bible school, MYF, the choir, and my parents were in the men's and women's organizations. My mother sang a solo in the choir on the same day she took her life. Sometimes life does not make sense, especially when you are a thirteen-year-old overweight, nail-biting, insecure teenager. I reflect now and think, *Whoa, someone should have put the brakes on!*

I was saved when I was twelve. Remember I went with a friend to a Valentine's banquet for youth the Baptist Church was having. I had never heard the words that were spoken that night nor did I hear them again until much later. That night I got saved, and I went home to tell my mother. My mother never let me go to other denominations' church functions again. When she died on April 16, 1968, my dad never took us back to church either.

What I did not know was how to find the answers I sought, not in people or things or passing flings or passions. What I sought was in the Word of God. However, the Word of God was not familiar to me, and I sought my comfort elsewhere. Paul tells us in Ephesians 1:13–14:

> In Him you also trusted, after you heard the word of truth, the gospel of your salvation; to whom also, having believed, you were sealed with the Holy Spirit of promise, who, is the guarantee of our inheritance until the redemption of the purchased possession, to the praise of His glory.

So now I am sealed with the Holy Spirit. But I don't know what that is or who He is. Yet the God of the universe, the Son Jesus, and the Holy Spirit began a plan of protection over my life.

Ninth grade, Leroy Martin Jr. High, Raleigh, North Carolina

In the summer of 1968, after my mother died, I went to visit my aunt and uncle in North Carolina. I had a life that I was not accustomed to. I was thirteen and I could be a teenager. My aunt made me clothes or bought me clothes. I have to say I was a little spoiled. I went on weekend camping trips with a distant cousin (who I met while there). She was my age, and I went to church again. Toward the end of my two-month stay, I begged my father to let me stay and go to school. This year was the best year of my school years. I was an average student, but I was a student. There wasn't any fighting or verbal conflict interfering with me being a child. I had a birthday party, where new friends were invited, and they came. I thought I had arrived. I had never had a party before, except with family. The summer after ninth grade, my sister and brother came for a visit. We all loved it there, and I wanted to stay and go to high school. My dad sold the house and moved to another area of College Park, and he brought all three of us back to Georgia.

I was a normal kid, enjoying life and barely sneaking by with my grades. I had crying bouts, usually brought on by hormones. I was often compared emotionally to my mother. I could not convince the adults in my life that I would never harm myself, although I probably gave them good cause to fear with my bouts of depression and mood swings. Remember, I don't know what normal is. I have a very distorted ideal of the concept of normal.

Tenth grade, College Park High, College Park, Georgia

We lived one mile from school, just under the required distance to ride the bus. Dad would drop us off most mornings, but we had to walk home every afternoon. My sister was in the band and played basketball, so most days I walked by myself. The home was nice, but there were no neighbors with children. I fell into the role of being the replacement for my mother. My brother had learning disabilities, and he went to a school out of our area, so Dad dropped him off and picked him up every day. No one told me to play all the roles a mother typically plays. But Satan, ever whispering in my ears, was weighing me down with burdens I was never asked to bear. Jesus said in Matthew 11:28–30, "Come to Me all you who labor and are heavy laden, and I will give you rest. Take My yoke upon you and learn from Me, for I am gentle and lowly in heart, and you will find rest for your souls. For My yoke is easy and My burden is light."

I was the oldest and took over the spot that my mother left empty. No one really asked me to, but no one ever stopped me from becoming the cook, maid, babysitter, launderer, student, sister, and daughter to name a few roles. However, all this unwarranted responsibility took its toll on me emotionally. I was hanging out with the wrong crowd. I met a boy who showed me love and affection. I had a distorted view of what love and affection was. I began to let him teach me what love and affection was, and I was sinning against God. I began to smoke cigarettes. I was having a major burnout, and it was a wildfire that was burning out of control. I am not sure if my father knew what was going on or if he just could not face any more heartache.

I burned out mid-February 1970 and ran away from home. I wasn't too bright in decision-making during that time. I was so in love with this person that we began to tell people we were married. I was gone three months to places I should have never been exposed to. I was introduced to communal living and the drug scene; however, I never partook. I was also introduced to some obscene sexual practices when an old man tried to assault me; I was working in his shop under an alias. I forgot to mention that when I ran away, we took my dad's car. Another reason my dad was so mad at me. I would have never gone through with it, but the boy I left with had my keys, and I thought I would be in a lot of trouble if I didn't go with the car. He taught me how to drive because I had never driven on a road before. He had stolen a wallet from someone, and we charged the gas and oil. The car broke down in Gary, Indiana. I don't know what became of it.

We stayed with some strangers (hippies) before we hitchhiked to Pittsburgh, Pennsylvania, in the dead of winter. I wasn't too smart back then. I had on four layers of clothes, and I was so cold I wanted to lie down and die. But someone came along and picked us up and took us the remaining distance. It must have been ten degrees outside. I stole food and cigarettes. I saw with my eyes sin that would not glorify God to repeat. I didn't know it then, but God protected me every bad step I took because I was a *child of the King*. I just didn't know it. He still had a plan for me. He said He would never leave me nor forsake me. I had never heard this, but He protected me along the way.

My hormones were raging; my emotions were on my sleeve and running like a runaway train with no conductor. I kept telling myself that no one loved me, and no one would miss me. I was in love. I mean I was really in love. Although Satan had an influence on my life, I was trying to be the best girlfriend/wife that I could be. We were both fifteen and neither of us had a clue about grown-up life. It broke my heart to leave him and return home.

We are backing up a little. I had been working at a food plant which made salads that sell in grocery stores like potato salad, coleslaw, fruit salad, etc. I had the task of lifting large bags of potatoes or cabbages that were peeled or shredded. I had almost worked enough to get my first paycheck. I was on my way home one evening. We walked everywhere in Pittsburgh, so it took twenty to thirty minutes. I was about halfway home when he and a friend met me and said I could not go home. "Why?" I asked, and he said two men came to the door looking for me. He said they were dressed in black suits and looked like cops.

So for the next several hours, we walked around several neighborhoods and went into stores to get warm. It was close to ten before we ever thought it was safe enough to return home. I was afraid for the first time since I left. Who were these men, and where did they come from? As an adult, I can see similarities to Lot when God sent two angels to rescue him from Sodom. These men knew my name. How did they know?

I was afraid to go home because I did not have the car I had taken. I called my aunt in North Carolina called from a payphone and made the call collect to my aunt for her to pay for, and she sent me the money to come home on a bus. She told me not to contact my father because he said he would have me arrested on sight. Did God send angels to rescue me? I never saw them in person. Mid-April I returned to North Carolina as it was the safest place to return to. I had heard that my father was going to have me arrested on sight, so I wanted a haven to return to. I found out that my father was getting married in late April, and our family would grow again.

I was on an emotional roller coaster, and my mood swings were dark. I had given up what I thought was the love of my life to return home. God had protected me through the days and nights I was gone. I hitchhiked up and down the eastern United States but avoided North Carolina and Georgia for fear of being caught. God protected me from pregnancy, disease, and harm. The harm I received was seeing with my eyes, hearing with my ears, and participating in sexual intercourse prior to marriage. The lack of today's technology was on my side. I would have never gotten as far as I did then today.

When I arrived home, I found all my belongings had been packed up and stored in the hall closet. I guess my family wasn't expecting me to return. I did return, and I had to see a juvenile officer several times and go to a yearlong mandatory psychological therapy. I felt like a failure. I was not wanted at home, and I left the one person who had protected me and who I had loved. My goal was to survive until I was eighteen when I could make my own decisions.

One weekend, our parents allowed us to have a party. Remember my friends from College Park were not very good acquaintances, and my sister's friends were two years younger. My stepsister's friends were from another school (Walter F. George). We had three different sets and types of friends. The party was in our basement, where everyone who came in passed my parents. The party was huge, and there were people there that we didn't even know. At this point I was not even in school (because of coming home in the middle of the semester). Guess who got blamed the next day for all the liquor bottles and beer bottles in the basement and in the yard? If you guessed me, you would be right.

After I ran away, I got blamed for anything anyone did, even if I wasn't involved, because I was the bad child. So I was confronted with a loud cursing argument. My father was yelling and I was yelling and my father called me several unattractive names. I retorted with like words aimed at him, which started a physical beating of hair pulling, cursing, hitting, and kicking. He was angry, and I was to be blamed for his embarrassment over the party that his neighbors and new wife and new daughter had witnessed. This conflict began the part of my life where I was doing time until I was eighteen literally. Life was mostly miserable. I was sinking in quicksand, and there was no one to save me.

Eleventh and twelfth, Lakeshore High School, College Park, Georgia

My family moved again to another part of College Park, about a mile or two from the bus line. I went to summer school to make up the required courses to stay on track for eleventh grade. During that summer, my love returned to my life. He and some friends were renting an apartment near the school I was attending for summer school. I would walk there every day after school (12:00), and I would stay until the last minute for the last bus to take me to my pickup spot around five in the evening. Again, I was involved in activities unpleasing to God, but who was God to me? I didn't even think about sin. I was with my love, and my heart was full.

Toward the end of summer, I had to start my new high school, and my love was leaving the area. He begged me over and over to leave with him. Every day for about two weeks he would plead with me to leave with him. Something within me would not let me leave again. My heart was breaking and the love of my life was leaving and I may never see him again. I have never seen him again. My emotions swell up within me as I write this testimony. Although I had a distorted view of love and affection, I still had the capacity to give my whole heart to someone else. I hurt for the loss of him, and I regret the grieving of the Holy Spirit that I have participated in *the sin*.

I am not promoting the behavior of my past, but this is a testimony, and I want it to be truthful. In Ephesians 4:25–32, Paul talks about "not grieving the Holy Spirit of God, by whom you were sealed for the day of redemption." Forgiveness defeats unresolved conflict or anger. I do not need to be a poor witness to others, and I must get control of myself through the Holy Spirit. Paul is right! However, I didn't know Paul, let alone the Holy Spirit. My life was spiraling out of control.

I started my therapy at Georgia State University under a graduate program they offered every Thursday. I was in a mixed group of adults (male, female, and couples). It always felt odd because I needed to work out the emotional problems with my mother's death and yet I felt like an outsider. I wasn't really getting the therapy I needed. I always felt as if the adults did not want me there, but I was ordered to go or else go to juvenile. In fact, I was threatened with juvenile at every argument at home.

I would catch the bus to downtown Atlanta every Thursday and get off at Rich's. I would walk the distance to Georgia State University, about a mile or better, and then after the session I would walk head back to Rich's to ride the bus home. Most of the time I was walking in the dark on the streets of Atlanta, during an age of drugs and homeless people, and I remember being very afraid but trying to act casual waiting for the bus with all those strangers and drunks. I look back and wonder how I was able to make that journey by myself all that time. Did my family want me to run again, or maybe they didn't care enough about me to be concerned for my safety?

God's protection was with me every step I took. In 1 Corinthians 10:12–13, we are told that God provides a way of escape and protection. He placed guardian angels with me, and I didn't know it. I often wondered if this temporary freedom was given to me to run again and disappear. I didn't run physically, but my mind was not right. I was depressed and in very dark places. I was sad, and I was grieving the loss of my love.

I was able to attend two years at the same high school, Lakeshore High, in College Park, Georgia. I met a boy in my history class, and we dated throughout our junior and senior years. This relationship was not a healthy one. I was an emotional basket case, very depressed, and sad. It seemed like the harder I tried, the more trouble I stayed in. During my eleventh-grade year, I became very depressed. I wore no makeup, and I cried all the time. Most of my clothing was black.

I didn't care about my life yet I clung to the unhealthy physical relationship I had with my boyfriend.

In my junior year, my stepmother arranged for me to be evaluated by a child psychologist because she was trying to commit me to Georgia Regional Hospital. My brother was already there due to personality and behavioral problems. We had family counseling that usually ended with me getting blamed, and I would walk out and refuse to participate. My emotional state was not helping me. However, I went to the psychologist and was tested. I then spoke to the psychologist about his observations, and I could voice my feelings and frustrations. He told me that there was nothing wrong with me and that I was one of the most intelligent teenagers he knew. He spoke to my stepmother for a while. I don't know what was discussed with her, but I know that I never went back to any of the family sessions or his office again.

High school was full of dark, dark years and events that caused guilt, pain, and feelings of unworthiness. It is so hard to express just how depressed and oppressed I was. Some was due to the bad decisions I was making, and some was caused by others. I think it was a miracle that I did not get into drugs and alcohol. I had other vices and sins. Satan had me in bondage, and I let him. Remember I was saved at the age of twelve; however, I did not have any spiritual growth or training. But what? God had a plan. I was oblivious to the plan, but God still had it!

Even though I was a Christian, God allowed me to have a free will. He allowed me to make mistakes and sin against His laws. I can't say it was because I didn't know, but I didn't know; I did not seek the Word, I did not seek God. I really forgot all about God and thought no one else thought my life was worthy, so I took my life and decisions into my own hands. I messed it up pretty good. If you saw me in action, you might say I was on the road to self-demise. I just could not make good decisions. What was to become of me?

I want to address why it is so important to wait for intimate relationships until marriage. God made man (Adam) and then He made woman from Adam's rib (Eve) to complement each other. All through the Bible, you can find accounts of God's commands on marriage and the purity of marriage. First Timothy 5:22 says, "Do not lay hands on anyone hastily, nor share in other people's sin; keep yourself pure." When we get ahead of God and enter into intimate relations with another person, we are making a covenant with that person. The importance of your first intimate experience is that it is the one you remember all your life. You may forget many loose or temporary relationships, but you will never forget your first. That one is very special, an expression of love between two people. Don't confuse actions of lust for love.

In my experience, I was in love, and I thought my world revolved around this person in my life. Today, fifty years later, I can see and feel every event from that first intimate relationship as if it were today. God wants us to protect us from harm and emotional hurt. He wants us to stand strong and persevere until marriage so that the first night as husband and wife, our gift to each other is our first and only covenant of intimacy to seal the covenant between each other. It's a binding covenant of love and commitment to each other.

When we sin and enter relations outside of marriage, we rob ourselves of the wondrous gift to each other. It is special, sweet, tender, passionate, and never-ending except when we have other relations with others. The special becomes ordinary, an act of lust, and a wanting of self-satisfaction that we can never find because we did not save ourselves for the one God had reserved for us.

Before you think I am just throwing out an unwarranted lecture on premarital sex, let me tell you my heartache. My first encounter was with the boy my same age, fifteen, and we were on the run. We made it to a friend's house in Indiana, and she let us stay a couple of days. She was a little older than I was, and she was married and was expecting their first child. We told them we eloped and got married in Ringgold, Georgia. This person and I made a commitment to each other, a pledge of love. Then we consummated and sealed the commitment. We were children and could not foresee the future and the many, many trials we would encounter. My heart aches knowing that God's blessings were being missed. Jeremiah 29:11 says, "I know the plans I have for you, says the Lord, plans for peace and not of evil, to give you a future and a hope…"

God's hand of protection was on me, even though I had wandered off His path. He even used the person with me to protect me. There were several times along the road that He could have left me, but He always took care of me. God uses the broken, the sinners, the people with abuse and scars to do His work, even if the one He is protecting is outside His will. An intimate act, a fleeting moment outside of God's plan, can haunt you for the rest of your life, especially if you squandered God's gifts and blessings for brief satisfaction.

Psalm 25 talks about deliverance and forgiveness. Verse 4 says, "Show me Your ways O Lord; teach me Your paths. Lead me in Your truth, and teach me; for You are the God of my salvation…" I was saved at twelve, and the Holy Spirit lived in my heart. However, I was not concerned because I did not know about the Holy Spirit. Even in our deepest despair, God hears the groans of the Holy Spirit on our behalf. Verse 11 says, "For your name's sake, O Lord, pardon my sin, for it is great." God has more grace and mercy than we do, and He does forgive just because we ask. He is merciful. He gave His One and only Son, Jesus, that we may come through Him to heaven.

CHAPTER 3

My son, do not forget my law, but let your heart
keep My Commands; for length of days and long
life and peace they will add to you…

—Proverbs 3:1–8

I GRADUATED FROM high school barely passing. My SAT scores were 650 combined. I know, not too good. I wanted to go to nursing school, and I had chosen Grady School of Nursing to apply to. I did not make the cut. My stepmother went with me to the interview. I felt very insecure and really stupid. My stepmother sent my information to Abraham Baldwin Agriculture College (ABAC). Ratio of boys to girls was ten to one. I am a city girl from Atlanta, stuck in South Georgia two hundred miles from home.

I was sent to college about three weeks after graduating from high school. I was seventeen. I had no control over my life. My parents signed the forms that stated I could not have a part-time job or leave campus overnight without their permission. I also could not go home, even if sick, without their permission. My classes were 11:00 a.m. then 12:00 to 1:00 then 6:00 p.m. The cafeteria was open at six to eight every morning, twelve to one for lunch, and six to seven every evening for dinner. I was given a card for meals paid for by my parents; however, I was not able to use it because of the class times. I received $5.00 per week for allowance. I did not receive my allowance for a period of time because I owed $50.00 to my dad that was not used for books. I could babysit for professors, but I could not have a *job*.

I was told to get up and eat breakfast, which would give me one meal a day. How many seventeen-year-olds get up for breakfast when their first class isn't until 11:00 a.m.? I was hungry a lot. I would do laundry for the guys, so I could throw in my laundry. I would offer to cook for guys that lived off campus if they bought the food, so I could eat. I was in survival mode.

My parents had passed through Tifton and visited for about thirty minutes on their way home from the family vacation to Disney World. I have yet to visit Disney World. They said it was the only time they could go, but they gave me their leftover bread, peanut butter, and other items I can't remember. I missed the family vacation, but I got the leftovers. That's what I felt like—a leftover.

God was still in control, but I couldn't see it.

During the semester change of summer and fall, all non-international students were required to leave campus. My parents would not come and get me and told me to find my own way home. I was not wanted. I was able to get a ride home. My stepmother called my housemother to confirm I had to vacate the campus.

I had broken up with my high school boyfriend over the summer, but during the break, we got back together. Needless to say, I was taking control of my life. I was reckless in my decisions, and I abandoned any realization that anyone cared what happened to me. I still had an 11:30 curfew, but my two sisters did not have a curfew. This confirmed my belief that I would always be punished for decisions made years earlier. I caught a ride back to school with my belongings. My parents did not even make the time to take me back to school. I did not know that my stay would be brief because I was pregnant.

I met my oldest and dearest friend, Betty Jo Martin, during that short stay at ABAC. We have been friends for over forty years. She is the reason I went to ABAC. I failed every class. I dropped out of college in late October and came home to get married. It was supposed to be a small church wedding, with family and a few friends. However, when my parents found out I was pregnant, my wedding was cancelled, and I was lectured on how embarrassing I was for the condition I was in. "What would my dad's associates think?" I didn't know nor did I care. My world was crumbling around me, and this time, I added to the chaos.

There was never any concern for me. My stepmother controlled and influenced my father. I was considered the bad child, and it was evident from the mess I had made of my life. I was only home two short years from my excursion across the country, but I would pay for it most of my life. This probably explains why I am an overachiever in everything I attempt. Always trying to prove my worth, so someone would be proud of me. Little did I know, God was still working and molding me. He crushed my heart and began to remold me into something or someone He could use one day to spread the story of His redemption.

CHAPTER 4

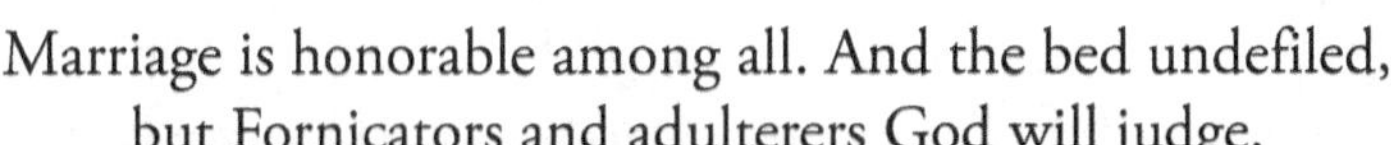

Marriage is honorable among all. And the bed undefiled,
but Fornicators and adulterers God will judge.

—Hebrews 13:4

I TRIED TO make the best of my situation. I got married, and we moved within two blocks of a small shopping center, where I got a part-time job at W.T. Grants. I was to work through Christmas, but I stayed until May. The office manager knew I was young, and she trained me for bookkeeping. This basic skill took me to future jobs, but it was the foundation. Mrs. Sikes was the manager's name, and I am grateful she mentored me in the basics of bookkeeping and office work. In 1972 and 1973, pregnant women would typically lose their jobs because they were pregnant. She kept me, and she taught me. God still had His plan. I was still oblivious to it!

We moved to another part of College Park, Georgia and rented an apartment. We were the only ones married out of all our friends. I only had one or two girlfriends, where my husband had a lot of dope-smoking, drug-taking, drinking buddies. He was always gone on the weekends with the guys. I would go to bed on Saturday night and wake up on Sunday morning and not know who may be asleep in the living room.

One weekend my husband and a friend decided to sell weed. They bought eight pounds from a local dealer to redistribute. However, during the buy, an undercover officer called in the troops, and both were arrested right there in the front parking lot. They went to trial and both were sentenced and the friend was sent to jail. My husband was fined and sentenced to probation.

It would be about six years after I was saved, under the persuasion of my dear mother-in-law, that I would start back to church with my daughter. I began to hear the grounded Word of God in such a way I soaked up the scripture like a sponge soaks up water. I was hungry for the Word. God did have a plan for my life.

Although God had a plan for my life, Satan also had a plan. Satan set out to destroy me. I was married at the age of eighteen and had my daughter within the year. God blessed me with the most beautiful and smartest daughter. She had such a sweet spirit, always smiling and loving. Her father never really wanted to be married with the commitment of a family, but marriage is what people did when you find yourself pregnant in 1972. The alternative was abortion or adoption, neither of which I believed in. I was married almost eight years when we divorced and went our separate ways. I remained close to my husband's family; after all, I did not divorce them. I stopped going to church after my divorce because I knew the way the church felt about divorce. The deacons came to see me and tried to convince me to stay with the marriage, but I told them I had been through counseling. This was the second time I had filed for divorce. I had given up on this marriage.

Marriage #2

I met someone through my workplace. We met for dinner a couple of times. I was almost divorced from my first husband, and I had moved in with my parents for about a month, waiting to find a place to live. There was a lot of tension between my stepmother and myself. We argued a lot. She thought I should have stayed with my soon-to-be ex-husband. Remember I have distorted views of love, affection, and acceptance.

The stress was too great at my parents'. I would fix dinner or pick up something, but my stepmother quit coming home until later because I was there. The man I was seeing after work asked me to move in with him. I only cleared about $400.00 per month, and I already knew it would be difficult to provide for my daughter. My child support started out at $150.00 per month. I saw an opportunity, and I said yes.

I didn't even tell my parents where I had moved for about six months. No one cared what happened to me, so why do I need to tell them where I live now? During this time period, I started back to school. I was twenty-six, and I had a seven-year-old in second grade. I went to school during the evening and worked during the day.

My ex-husband wanted to marry his girlfriend in the church where we had been members. The church said no because of their stand on divorce. He got very angry at them and told them I was living with someone and gave them my address. The deacons came to see me again, and I told them I did not want to speak to them. I received a call from a close friend whose husband was a deacon at the church I previously attended. I was informed that my name would be read before the church and my name removed from the membership rolls. I told her that if that church felt they needed to side with someone who told lies and who had previously had many, many relationships while married, they needed to do what they felt they needed to do. So I was now removed from the church membership.

We lived together three years before marrying in September 1983. We bought a house and moved across town to Woodstock, Georgia. We were active in our neighborhood, and I continued to complete my undergraduate studies. I was active in local and state politics. I went to church some, but I was ridiculed by my husband when I attended. He was not a Christian, even though he was a good citizen. During our sixth year of marriage, he told me he had wasted ten years of his life. He was not where he had envisioned himself at the age of forty. He wasn't there most of the time. I got very angry, and I began to build walls around my heart. Satan was thrilled as I took out my anger in bad decisions and a sinful adulteress relationship with someone from work. It was only temporary, and I regret every action during that time period. I cannot live in my past regrets; I asked for forgiveness from God. My marriage was over, and I felt cast aside again.

We were married seven years to the day when our divorce went through. I had completed almost four years of college by this time. After our divorce, we continued to see each other until the year I graduated from Kennesaw State, 1992. He broke my heart at Thanksgiving of 1992 when he broke off our relationship completely. I went through a deep grieving over this.

I looked at my life and wondered why I was so vile and unworthy. I had tried to please all of my spouses, yet they all either dated other women or cast me aside and conveyed I had wasted their time. What a failure I had become. There must be no hope for me.

CHAPTER 5

For your Maker is your husband, the Lord of hosts is His
Name; and your Redeemer is the Holy One of Israel; He is
called the God of the whole earth. For the Lord has called
you Like a woman forsaken and grieved in spirit. Like a
youthful wife when you were refused; says your God.

—Isaiah 54:5–6

I STARTED READING some Christian books on how to deal with life better or how to rely on God's promises. I read one by Robert Schuler about prayer and how we should claim what we need in the name of Jesus, and He will answer our prayers. I also read a very good biography or autobiography about Helen Steiner Rice and how she was saved.

During this time, a lady that worked in the same office I did had been praying for me. Her name was Carolyn, and she was a praying woman. She had added my name to a prayer box in a prayer group she attended. On September 13, 1991, her prayer group met, and they drew my name out of the box to pray for. Carolyn was not present that night, and no one knew who I was or why I needed prayer. One of the ladies volunteered to sit in a chair and the remaining ladies laid hands on the one sitting in for me, and they began to pray. The next day, I was cleaning house when I thought, *I think I'll go to church tomorrow. If I go to church, I may as well go to Sunday school as well. Oh, but I won't tell Kris, my daughter, in case I change my mind.*

Kris had to work that Sunday, and she would never know if I went or did not go. So on Sunday, September 15, 1991 (my birthday), I went to church where Kris had been attending, Wildwood Baptist. I did not know one person there, but I went to Sunday school. The lesson was on Elijah and how he was favored by God. Next, I went to church, and I sat in the back, so no one would notice me. The first song to be sung was the doxology; I heard this all my life in the Methodist Church. God pricked my heart, and I cried through every song. The message was out of James and the dangers of self-sufficiency. I could not wait to get down the aisle and rededicate my life to a stranger, in a church where I knew no one. I began to work with other ladies in this church to develop a women's ministry. I joined this church, Wildwood Baptist, in Acworth, Georgia. I was in a lady's class, and then later I joined a single's class. I was active in Bible studies and facilitated several of Beth Moore's studies.

God always meets us where we are, and He uses special memories sometimes to prick our heart and make them tender for His glory to be revealed. God took a combination of early childhood memory of the doxology and the teaching I had received in an earlier church to bring about a redemptive spirit in me.

Mid-1993, Satan sent a person into my life to destroy it. I had been working in a small one-girl office, doing customer service and accounting. This person was a purchasing clerk for one of our clients. We would chat almost daily about orders and deliveries. We had conversations for about six months when we decided to meet in person. It was an awkward meeting. He showed up at my house one day with fish he had caught. We went to lunch, and I drove because his car was full of trash. I mean *full of trash*. This was the first *red* flag. However, he kept coming around and before you know it, he's there all the time.

My closest friend and buddy, Nancy, stopped coming around as much. Second *red* flag and I continued down the road to no return. Before long I was blatantly absent from church. I only showed up when I had made obligations for the women's ministry events. My friends Julie W. and LaSydia P., who I started the women's ministry with, would call every Saturday to ask about me coming to church.

They would not ask questions about my present life, but they always reminded me that God loved me, and they were praying for me.

My daughter had met her husband, and they had started dating. Then they started talking about getting married. I started thinking about the wedding and what my life looked like. I was not happy with myself. I began praying to God to remove this person from my life. I did not think I was emotionally capable of ending the relationship. I asked Julie to pray for me, and I told her I needed help from God, but I did not reveal what the request was.

This person who befriended me was someone I allowed in my life. Why did I always set myself up to settle for less than what God had intended? I was seeing a little less of this person because all the wedding planning and stuff was not his thing. I look back now and realize that God was slowly removing him from my life. I found out that my daughter was pregnant, and we moved up her wedding date to January. This fit well with God's plan because I started thinking I did not want my grandchild to ask questions or see me smoke (that's right, I had started back smoking—red flag).

One day, this person called and said they were coming by that night. I decided right there that I would fix a grilled steak dinner, and after, I would break the relationship off. What could happen? I didn't think he would harm me. After dinner, I said I needed to talk with him about something that had been bothering me. (In his absence, I had started back to church.) I told him that we could be friends or we could go to the movies or out to dinner. But under no circumstances could he stay overnight any longer. He looked up at me and said, "I was wondering what took you so long."

That was the last time I ever saw him. He disappeared from my life almost as quickly as he entered it.

This person was raised in a Baptist church. I had met his parents and siblings. They were a nice family, but his values *never* came close to mine. However, I was blinded by the desire to be wanted and needed. His values were in pornographic movies, alcohol, fishing, and hunting. I was never on the list. I was blinded by the fact that I had been married twice and divorced twice and was a complete failure in relationships. I prayed to God that if He helped me get out of the relationship, I would be satisfied with just Him. Praise God. I repented to God and to my friends.

At this point in my life, I was consumed with my daughter's wedding. Then I started taking Bible studies and began walking a journey of spiritual healing. God sent along a spiritual mentor, Frances W., to church who helped me for several years. We walked together and had dinner; we attended church and choir together. I got some Christian counseling that began to change the way I viewed myself.

What an idea! I had the whole picture of my life wrong. My counselor introduced me to Psalm 139. I had never read this before nor had this been explained to me. In Psalm 139 it states, "You have searched me and known me." Wow! God knew everything about me, my coming and going, and He understood my thoughts. Boy was I in trouble. "Your hand is upon me." "I am fearfully and wonderfully made." "Your eyes saw my substance, being yet unformed and in Your book, they were all written. The days fashioned for me, when as yet there were none of them." God created me just the way He wanted me. He touched me, and He made me whole. Psalm 139:23–24 says, "Search me O God and know my heart. Try me, and know my anxieties, and see if there is any wicked way in me and lead me in the way everlasting."

God saw all the gummy, smelly, scum I had chosen or had chosen for me, and He made me any way. Just the way I am is the character-building school of sin, regrets, and redemption He allowed in my life because when I was just twelve, I said I needed to be saved from sin and myself. All those years of protection flooded back before me today, and I thank God for His mercy and grace on my life. I could have been killed, addicted, abused, and incarcerated had it not been for His protection on my life.

Now before you think I am all perfect now, I am not. If it were not for Jesus and the cross He bore, I would not be writing this testimony. I began praying Psalm 37:4, "Delight yourself in the Lord, and He will give you the desires of your heart." Also Matthew 6:33, "But seek first the kingdom of God and His righteousness, and all these things shall be added to you." I prayed to God His promise in

Joel 2:25, "So I will restore to you the years that the swarming locust has eaten." This is the promise I stood on then and I stand on today.

I am not innocent in some of my circumstances. I chose some out of ignorance, out of anger and rebellion, and some out of selfishness. I don't want to go into too many details because it does not glorify God to expose every nasty little detail of my life or those who played a part. I was bound by Satan through sinful sexual relationships. Every relationship I had in my past was based on lust, sex, adultery, and self-pleasure. Remember I would take control over my life, and I was the only one who could make it better.

It glorifies God to know that I have grown to love Him more and more every day and that I have been redeemed from sin and myself. My counselor once told me that the way we see ourselves is based on 80 percent lies—lies we have been told and lies we tell ourselves. He was right. I listened to myself too long. I was leading a Beth Moore Bible study, *Breaking Free*, when Beth described our lives before becoming a Christian as one in chains locked in jail cell. Once we accept Christ as our Lord and Savior, the chains are removed, and the cell door is opened. However, many of us remain in the cell, too afraid to experience the freedom we now have through Christ. This spoke volumes to me and who I was in Christ. I was a child of God, a princess in the royal line redeemed by the blood of Christ Jesus.

I had lived for years in a depressed state of mind. I never *felt* loved. I didn't say I wasn't loved; I said I never felt loved. There was a lot of verbal fighting and abuse in my family. I carried unwarranted guilt from my mother's death and the last words I had spoken to her. She was a person who I could never please. I always had a feeling of failure and great disappointment. It always seemed the harder I tried to please all those around me, the deeper my hole became. Once I understood who I was in God's eyes and under the salvation provided by the blood of Jesus, I began a slow walk of healing. This is an ongoing process that God is always working on me. However, the initial walk of healing began with several Bible studies. The first was *To Live Is Christ* about the life of Paul, *A Heart Like His* about King David, then *Living Beyond Yourself*, the fruit of the spirit. *Breaking Free* was the ultimate look at the distorted view I had of my life and of myself (all Beth Moore studies).

Let me stress that no matter what we feel like or how unworthy our life seems, nothing can change the fact that God loves us so much that He sent His one and only Son to die on the cross to redeem our souls (John 3:16). The only thing we need to do is accept His Son as our Lord and Savior. Seems too simple. It is. We humans somehow have a need to complicate everything we attempt. God made salvation simple, and all He wants is our acceptance and to come just as we are.

I felt the call to missions during our first mission's conference in 1999. I went on my first mission trip in June of 2000 to Malawi, Africa. I knew missions were my life. I was on fire for Africa. When the opportunity came up to go a second time in 2002 to Ghana, I jumped at the chance to go. I was so moved by the mission's conference in 2001 that I committed publicly to the call to missions on my life. I began to campaign for long-term missions acceptance through the Southern Baptist Mission Board. I mean to tell you I had my application in and about six deacons and pastors wrote letters of recommendations for me. I was campaigning for my cause. I was on the way to Africa. I was campaigning, I was going, my cause, and on and on the I's went. Remember the old song "I Did It My Way"? That was what was happening—I was doing everything my way and not waiting on God.

CHAPTER 6

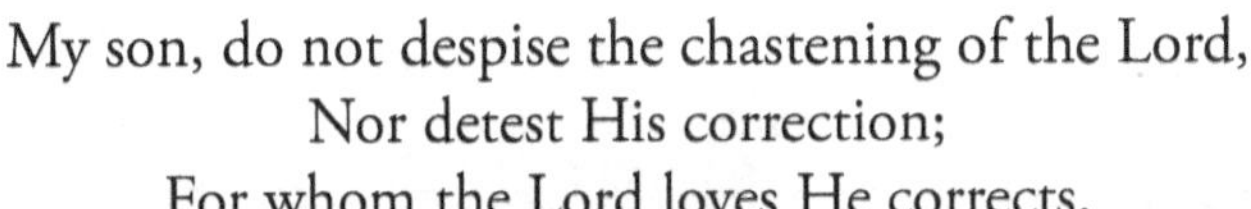

My son, do not despise the chastening of the Lord,
> Nor detest His correction;
For whom the Lord loves He corrects.
>>   —Proverbs 3:11–12

AFTER I RETURNED from Ghana in February 2002, I heard from an old neighborhood friend from thirty years ago. He is two years younger than I am, and he was a part of the neighborhood crowd. We all hung out together, but there was never any interest in him. After all, he was younger than me even if he was cute. We began to talk and converse on the phone. I had sold my house before my trip to Ghana, and I had made plans to move into a friend's guest room. I was moving on April 1, 2002, and my house would close the following week. My long-lost friend and I rekindled our friendship and here goes Mary's head again.

I move into his apartment across town, and I don't move into the friend's guest room. Within twenty-four hours, my friends and my mentor had found me. They came to take me back to Kennesaw. I was stubborn and did not go. My actions severed our friendships. I began to receive phone calls and messages, cards, and letters about my sin and the fact I had turned my back on God. I had not turned my back on God; I had been influenced by someone who did know me in the past, who accepted me and all my flaws to care about me. At this point in my life, I had been single for twelve years. We lived together for about one year when he asked me to marry him. I said yes, and we married on June 12, 2003.

It was shortly after getting married I was led to attend Rockdale Baptist Church. I had decided that I would not get ahead of God by volunteering for every project in town to satisfy my need for acceptance. My new husband was very forthright when he said, "You know you will never leave the county again?"

We had arguments over this issue several times. I would cry over a movie or book that involved missions, and he would feel pressured to make his stand again. I kept my mouth shut. I promised him I would never ask to go anywhere I already knew he would not let me go.

I joined a Sunday school class, the Sonshine Class, led by Delores Biddy. What a wonderful class, and I began to get involved with missions. I had not joined the church because my husband had indicated he did not want me to join. I was asked to serve on the mission's team, but I was not a church member. I came home and told Mike that I had been asked to serve on the mission's team, and did he mind? He indicated that I would never go on any trip, but I could serve as long as I never expected to go out of the country again. I told my husband that I needed to join the church, so I could serve on the committee, and his response was, "I thought you were already a member." I could hardly wait until the next Sunday to get here, so I could officially join Rockdale Baptist. Once again, I kept my mouth shut.

I had a peace that one day I would again go to Africa to serve again, but this time I would do it God's way. So I served on the committee and helped with the conference. I was happy to be attending church again. My husband did not attend, but he encouraged me to go. He never once ridiculed me for my beliefs. In fact, my husband is a Christian. I truly believe he was sent by God to be a part of my life. He stopped my process of long-term serving in missions, or maybe it was God who stopped my process. Notice I said my process. God was not ready for me to serve in that capacity.

Mike is who God allowed in my life. I had been single for twelve years when Mike and I reconnected. Neither one of us was looking to date or enter into any relationship. We have many conversations about God, and His Son, Jesus. Mike is a Christian, but he does not attend church. In the beginning, he did not support my missionary spirit, but God has changed his heart. I believe that Mike and I were meant to be together, and that while we may have started out backward, God has helped us to grow as a married couple. My husband is my encourager, best friend, and mate. I prayed often to God the promise in Psalm 37:4, "Delight yourself in the Lord, and He will give you the desires of your heart." I just did not realize how much my desires were to be wife and mother, and He blessed me with one more chance. That's what I love about God; He is the God of second, third, fourth chances.

I decided I wanted to go to Georgia State and earn my master's in education and get certified to teach history. Mike gave me full support, and in June of 2006 I quit my perfectly good job and began school full time. I was still serving on the missions committee during this time. One evening, I was working on homework before leaving for a missions meeting. Mike came in and said, "You know this schooling and your grades, and how everything has fallen into place is not by chance. I think God is going to use you and your teaching degree in the future. You know, once you graduate and get a teaching position, I guess you can go back to Africa with your friends to the orphanage they are building."

To say I was floored was an understatement. I casually and calmly said goodbye and left for my missions meeting. As I drove out of the apartment parking lot, I was shouting to the Lord, praising His name and the blessing He had just given me. God was changing Mike's heart about me going on a mission trip, and God did it all. He did not need my mouth or tears. I waited patiently on the Lord, and He provided.

I graduated in August 2007 from Georgia State with my master's in education and certification to teach sixth- to twelfth-grade history and geography. Another thing Mike said was once I had a job, I could sponsor a child at the Living Hope Center in Kenya. So we have been sponsoring Belinda since about September 2007. In January of 2009, Julie W. and Ethel C. from Living Hope Ministries stayed in our home, and they participated in the mission's conference at Rockdale Baptist. Mike saw who Julie and Ethel really were through their visit. Julie and Ethel encouraged me to sign up for the trip that June 2009. I asked Mike and he said, 'I don't really like that idea."

I reminded him of his statement about returning with my friends after I graduated and was teaching. God had changed Mike's heart, and I was on my way to Africa again. Wow, what an awesome God we serve.

CHAPTER 7

I will restore to you the years the locust have eaten.

—Joel 2:25

THE RELATIONSHIP I have today is totally different from what you have just read. My high school boyfriend is the father of my daughter. His mother, Retha, was sent to be a part of my life by God. I started dating him at sixteen. Because I had a mean-spirited sister and stepsister (they were teenagers), I was constantly under the threat of having my recent past exposed to my new boyfriend. You know, the fact that I had run away in tenth grade with a boy! The fact that I was always in trouble with my parents; maybe I wasn't so innocent to have as a girlfriend. I nipped that in the bud very quickly. I told my new boyfriend all the dirty secrets, but he still wanted to date me. The news that I wasn't innocent any longer quickly led to a physical relationship. Remember I have a distorted view of love and affection, filled with lust, not love.

During the end of my junior year, I was on the prom committee. The committee even chose the theme I had suggested, "Somewhere Over the Rainbow." I was very excited about going to prom. My boyfriend had already graduated, and he was returning for the event. Well, during spring break, my aunt and uncle came in from North Carolina, and they brought my distant cousin, Nancy, with them. She stayed with us, and we planned a night on the town. I had arranged to get some liquor (through my older stepsister). Bad news. Guess who told on me!

We all went to the drive-in for the first feature of the movie. We then went to Underground Atlanta to see the sights. Afterward, we grabbed something to eat at Shoney's in College Park. There was Nancy, my sister Barbara, Carl (Barbara's friend), George (friend), Don (my boyfriend), and me. My other stepsister did not come because she liked George, and she thought I had hooked him up with Nancy. We had previously gotten permission to stay out until 1:00 a.m. instead of midnight because of all the places we were going. My stepmother had given permission for this exception. My dad was still at work. So when we returned at 12:55 from all of our excursions, my dad and stepmother were waiting for us in the kitchen. Remember the alcohol? Well, I had consumed some and was a little tipsy. My parents were hopping mad and said we were late. We explained we had gotten permission from my stepmother, but she denied giving permission. I was grounded for thirty days. I missed my prom.

I became deeply depressed during this time period. This is when the psychological testing and family counseling sessions took place. I looked at family counseling as *jump Mary sessions*. During this same time period, I got suspended from school for smoking in the bathroom. Boy did I get the lectures about smoking. My stepmother smoked, but she was an adult. I was tired of getting all the blame, even if some were true. I told about how my sister and stepsister bummed cigarettes from me as fast as we were out of sight of our parents. I was told that was different; they did not do it at home. The rules in the house were in two sets, one for everyone else and one for Mary. I was approaching my last year in high school, and I was counting down the days.

Upon graduation, I received several gifts, but one was a Bible from my boyfriend's parents (Retha and Lester Loyd). I was a little offended because I was given a Bible. It sat on the shelf in the closet for about six months. Remember I had the shotgun wedding in the den at home, so no one would know. The day I got married, my stepmother asked for the house key back because I didn't need it any longer. I have never had a key to my parent's house since that day.

My new mother-in-law turned out to be my adversary and prayer partner. She took care of me after Kris was born. She encouraged me to visit her church and bring Kris. I went alone most of the time to Sunday school and church. I joined the church and was baptized (for the third time), and I was semi-happy. During the early years of my marriage, I was having difficulty dealing with a lot of things. Mrs. Loyd talked to me about getting counseling. She said she knew I wasn't crazy, like I was told, but that I needed some Christian counseling. This counseling was also marriage counseling. My husband went one time, and during that session, he told the counselor that he was going to leave me and that he did not want to be married. I was in about year three or four of that marriage. I continued to go for the sessions Mrs. Loyd had paid for. It helped me some.

It was the Basic Youth Conflicts Conference by Bill Gothard that changed some of my point of view. My first conference was when I was about twenty. He talked about conflicts that kept Christians bound up living defeated lives. Mr. Gothard spoke about forgiveness and forgiving others. He gave real-life examples of how to reconcile with people in our lives. In about year three or four, I sat down and wrote a tear-stained letter to my father asking for his forgiveness and forgiving him for the feelings I felt. I also wrote one to my stepmother. This is really when my relationship began to change with my parents. After all, I had the only grandchild, so they wanted a better relationship. I recently found out that my stepmother did not deliver the letter to my father. So I explained to him why I had written to him, and I was sorry he did not receive it.

Mrs. Loyd had always shown me unconditional love, the love that Christ shows all of us. I have almost worn out the Bible she gave me in 1972. She helped set up my apartment and taught me how to be a wife and mother. I praise God for every day she is in my life. We are still very close, and she introduces me as her best friend.

As for my parents, my stepmother has passed away and my father recently turned ninety. She had congested heart failure and some dementia. My father was her caregiver, and hospice nurses came by twice a week. I stepped in to help my father with issues concerning my adult brother. He has mental issues and needed some medical diagnosis recently. I went down several times a month to help care for my stepmother, so Dad could take care of errands and business. My dad and I have had many private conversations during the months of her illness, and I learned something very interesting. I had been told all my life by many family members that I was like my mother, and at one point that I was emotionally unstable like she was. However, I discovered I am more like my dad than I ever imagined.

You see, my father was a tormented man with demons from his childhood that haunted him into his adulthood. He married a damaged and abused woman. They proceeded to try to have a normal life. I love my father today, and I know he loves me. I also love all my siblings. The difference today is I have Christ's forgiveness and His mercy and strength to assure me of my place in His kingdom. Considering what my father had endured in his life, I think he did okay, or the best he could. In time, God healed many of the hurts. My father is a good man who had been married for forty-three years at that time. He was married seventeen years to my real mother. He nor my mother had any parenting skills because they never observed good parenting skills in their lives. I have forgiven them, and I have asked for forgiveness as well. Remember, I am not totally innocent in my circumstances.

As I said in the beginning, this story is not to place blame on anyone. This is just a story of my life journey that the Father of all creation allowed in my life to build character, compassion, and mercy for His dying world. He desires to have everyone saved and redeemed by Jesus's blood, but He also desires for all who are broken to be mended. My life reminds me of the potter's wheel, where the potter shapes and molds the vessel. Then when a weak spot emerges, the potter crushes the vessel and begins to reshape and smooth until it is perfected. God does that in our lives. He works on us and tests us, but He does not tempt us. Satan is the only one who tempts us. Temptation always involves sin; however, testing involves the building of endurance. Isaiah 40:31 states, "But those who wait on the Lord Shall renew their strength; they shall mount up with wings like eagles, they shall run and not be weary, they shall walk and not faint."

I wonder sometimes what life might have been like if my mother had not left us. Someone asked me one time if I could go back and change anything in my life, would I change anything? I told them I would change nothing. God had allowed every event in my life and every event and circumstance to help make me who I am today. I would not change one thing; I might make things worse than they were. I try and not live in my past regrets.

God has also sent me some very dear friends along the way. Some to whom I can never repay the kindness and generosity they have shown me. These are still dear friends today, although I don't see some any longer and some I see rarely. They are eternal friends, and for eternity, we will see each other and worship the Lord together. My advice to anyone is choose your friends carefully because they can lift you up in the Lord or tear you down for Satan. Several of my friends were sent to specifically walk with me during my initial healing journey. One told me one time (when I was falling apart), "Okay, you've had your pity party and cried. Get over it! Come back to reality." I was shocked and stopped cold in the middle of my pity party. Ecclesiastes 3:1–8 reminds us that "to everything there is a season. A time for every purpose under heaven…" God had a plan, and God has a plan for me and everyone else He has created.

During my journey of healing under the Master's guidance, I attended a women's conference at Calloway Gardens where Beth Moore was the keynote speaker. She spoke on Jesus's time in the garden of Gethsemane, just before His arrest. The example can be found in Matthew 26:36–46. Jesus left His three closest friends to watch and pray while He went further still to God. A place of further still is a place we go alone to our Father. A place where we are intimate with our Father, and a place where our friends cannot go with us. God has sent many friends during my walk, but my healing was because I went further still to my Father's arms where only He could touch me and heal me.

CHAPTER 8

Trust in the Lord with all your heart.
And lean not on your own understanding;
In all your ways acknowledge Him,
And He shall direct your path.

—Proverbs 3:5–6

GOD IS STILL working on me, and I thank Him for that. I was complaining one time about how bad things were in my life and the struggles I was going through facing the circumstances of my past, when my mentor reminded me, "Well, aren't you lucky because God chose you to work on today? He could have chosen anyone, but He chose you."

She had a way of making a person see the obvious. I still love and appreciate her today. I don't see her anymore, but boy do I quote her a lot. God gives us friends and mentors for the seasons in our life. Sometimes they are lifelong friends and sometimes they pass through until we meet again in eternity. Friends that God sends and uses are always friends forever.

I am in the middle of a doctoral program on curriculum, instruction, and assessment through Walden University. That's right, the girl who barely got out of high school went to college and graduated with a 3.33 GPA. In my master's program, I earned a 3.88 GPA, and I hold (at present) a 4.00 GPA in my doctorate program. God had all the capability in me the whole time. He equips each one of us for everything He wants to accomplish in our lives. I am also making plans to return to Kenya after graduation, which is about one year away.

I recently completed a Beth Moore Bible study on James, and I was convicted to stop stalling and write my testimony. A couple of friends have been prodding me, but I have stayed away because of fear. You heard it right—fear. Where does fear come from? Fear does not come from God. My grandmother Bryant's favorite verse in the Bible was Isaiah 41:10, "Fear not, for I am with you; be not dismayed, for I am your God. I will strengthen you. Yes, I will help you. I will uphold you with My righteous right hand." Wow! God was there all along. Every day I thought I was alone and lost, He was there protecting each hair on my head. He had a purpose for my life that I could not see. Jeremiah 32:17 says, "Ah, Lord God! Behold, You have made the heavens and the earth by Your great power and outstretched arm. There is nothing too hard for You." Praise God; there is nothing too hard for Him.

Isaiah 55 is full of God's promises. Verse 3 states, "Delight yourself in abundance. Incline your ear and come to Me. Listen, that you may live; and I will make an everlasting covenant with you." God wants a covenant with us. Verse 6 says, "Seek the LORD while He may be found; Call upon Him while He is near." God makes Himself available to us. In verse 7, it tells us, "And let him return to the LORD and He will have compassion on him. For He will abundantly pardon." God forgives. In 8, one of my favorites, "For My thoughts are not your thoughts, nor are your ways My ways." God knows all things. He knows the whole picture.

Verse 11 says, "So will My word be which goes forth from My mouth. It will not return to Me empty, without accomplishing what I desire." God speaks and He guides with His word. Verse 13 states, "It will be a memorial to the LORD. For an everlasting sign which will not be cut off." This is God's covenant. I had to ask myself, *Do I trust God enough to seek Him? Do I trust Him enough to forgive me? Do I trust Him enough to take care of me?* My answer had to be yes, yes, praise God, *yes*!

Jeremiah 29:11 says, "For I know the plans that I have for you, declares the LORD, plans for welfare and not for calamity to give you a future and a hope." The search for God's will begins with God. Who is God in my life? The search for God's will is built on His word. Second Corinthians 6:17 states, "The search for God's will is wrapped in prayer."

James 5:16 tells us, "Therefore confess your sins to one another and pray for one another so that you may be healed." God commands us to pray that we may be healed. There are many people who think healing is only physical, but God's healing is all-encompassing, and His healing is complete. God had performed a tremendous healing in my spirit. He still works on me daily and one day my healing will be complete and I will stand before my God and praise Him.

CHAPTER 9

I waited patiently for the Lord, and He inclined to me and heard my cry. He brought me up out of the pit of destruction, out of the miry clay, and He set my feet upon a rock, making my footsteps firm. He put a new song in my mouth, a song of praise to our God. Many will see and fear and will trust in the Lord.

—Psalm 40:1–3

This is what God did for me. I was on a long and broken road to destruction, and my feet were caught in the miry clay and muck of sin. He pulled me up and redeemed me and set my feet on His rock that I may be able to stand firm in Him. Praise God for the new song He put in my mouth, the song of salvation and praise. Only Jehovah Rapha (the God that heals) can accomplish this.

Isaiah 12:2 states, "Behold, God is my salvation. I will trust and not be afraid, for the Lord God is my strength and song."

Zach Williams has a song, "Fear Is a Liar," and the lyrics are so, so true:

> When he told you you're not good enough
> When he told you you're not right
> When he told you you're not strong enough
> To put up a good fight
> When he told you you're not worthy
> When he told you you're not loved
> When he told you you're not beautiful

That you'll never be enough
Fear, he is a liar
He will take your breath
Stop you in your steps
Fear he is a liar
He will rob your rest
Steal your happiness
When he told you were troubled
You'll forever be alone
When he told you you should run away
You'll never find a home
When he told you you were dirty
And you should be ashamed
When he told you you could be the one
That grace could never change
Fear he is a liar
He will rob your rest
Steal your happiness
Cast your fear in the fire
'Cause fear he is a liar

All my life had been lived listening to the evil one, the fallen angel Satan, the ruler of darkness. I never set out to follow him or his ways, but the further I stepped away from God the Father and Jesus Christ His Son, the further and deeper I was headed for hell.

In Psalm 37:1–2, 7–9, it says:

> Do not fret because of evildoers, be not envious toward wrongdoers. For they will wither quickly like the grass. Rest in the Lord and wait patiently for Him. Do not fret because of him who prospers in his way, because of the man who carries out wicked schemes. Cease from anger and forsake wrath; do not fret; it leads only to evildoing. For evildoers will be cut off, but those who wait for the LORD, they will inherit the land.

Fear does *not* come from God. We are not to fear evildoers because God will deal with those people. We are not to be envious of what they have, what they do, where they go, or how much money they make, and on and on. God is our provider, and the things evildoers have are all they have in this world because their judgment waits, and their reward will be eternity in hell if they deny the Savior. Remember: fear, he is a liar.

Another song caught my ear, and the words penetrated my conscious. The words are why I began the journey to write down my testimony and how God has healed me, or I should say how He is healing me. It's a lifelong process in everyone's life, especially mine. The song was by Selah, entitled "Bless the Broken Road."

> I set out on a narrow way, many years ago
> Hoping I would find true love, along the broken road
> But I got lost a time or two
> Wiped my brow and kept pushing through
> I couldn't see how every sign, pointed straight to you
> Every long lost dream led me to where you are
> Others who broke my heart, they were just northern stars
> Pointing me on my way, into your loving arms
> This much I know is true
> That god blessed the broken road
> That lead me straight to you…

Even though most of these words are true, and believe me, I had taken some bumpy, broken roads in my life, I decided that there are a couple of other songs and chorus that speak volumes about my journey with the Father of all healing, the Father of all creation, and the Almighty God. One in particular is by Travis Cottrell, and it is his remake on "Just as I Am."

> Just as I am, without one plea,
> but that thy blood was shed for me,
> and that thou bidst me come to thee,
> O Lamb of God, I come, I come.

Just as I am, and waiting not
to rid my soul of one dark blot,
to thee whose blood can cleanse each spot,
O Lamb of God, I come, I come.
Just as I am, though tossed about
with many a conflict, many a doubt,
fightings and fears within, without,
O Lamb of God, I come, I come.
Just as I am, poor, wretched, blind;
sight, riches, healing of the mind,
yea, all I need in thee to find,
O Lamb of God, I come, I come.
Just as I am, thou wilt receive,
wilt welcome, pardon, cleanse, relieve;
because thy promise I believe,
O Lamb of God, I come, I come.
Just as I am, thy love unknown
hath broken every barrier down;
now, to be thine, yea thine alone,
O Lamb of God, I come, I come.

New Chorus

I come broken to be mended I come wounded
to be healed
I come desperate to be rescued I come empty to
be filled
I come guilty to be pardoned by the blood of
Christ the Lamb
And I'm welcomed with open arms, praise God,
just as I am.

I remember this song all my life in the Methodist Church and the Baptist Church. This is the closing song at Billy Graham's conferences. A classic salvation song of all times, where I cry when I hear it.

Now that Travis Cottrell has written a chorus to go with it, the song is the epitome of my life and the healing work of God.

God does not need us. On the contrary, we need Him. He wants us just as we are. In Psalm 139, He tells us that we are fearfully and wonderfully made and that He knew all about us before He decided to make us. We humans are the ones with status needs and distorted thinking about what God wants. He wants us.

I, Mary, came broken to be mended by the blood of Christ the Lamb.

I, Mary, came wounded and brokenhearted to be healed by the blood of Christ the Lamb.

I, Mary, came desperate to be recused from myself and worldly influences.

I, Mary, come empty to be filled, with a deep filling and satisfying touch of Jesus.

I, Mary, come guilty, condemned, and on the road to hell, if not pardoned by the blood of Christ the Lamb.

I, Mary, am welcomed with open arms, from the only one who has *never* turned His back on me, praise God, just as I am.

I think about King David and Peter in the Bible. I am so glad God put them in the Bible. I also remember Rahab, Ruth, and Mary Madeline, all questionable women but redeemed by God. Rahab the harlot and Ruth the Moabite are in the lineage of Jesus, and Mary Madeline had demons cast from her. All were redeemed and all were welcomed with open arms just as they were. All had hearts for God.

God is still working on me. I am still broken, wounded, desperate, sometimes empty, and guilty. The difference today is I know where my strength, love, and acceptance can be found. Sometimes I battle with the old feelings of being unworthy, not loved, and not accepted. I have to stop and remind myself that those feelings are lies, and I am worthy, loved, and accepted because I have been created by God and redeemed by Christ His Son. In Mark 9:24 it states, "Help me in my unbelief." I have prayed that more than once for God to help me to believe in something, where my head knows what to believe but my heart is deceitful.

I come broken to be mended I come wounded
to be healed
I come desperate to be rescued I come empty to
be filled
I come guilty to be pardoned by the blood of
Christ the Lamb
And I'm welcomed with open arms, praise God,
just as I am.

In scripture, John 8:32 and 36 says, "You shall know the truth, and the truth shall make you free. Therefore, if the Son makes you free, you shall be free indeed." There is only one freedom and forgiveness, and that is from the Father through Jesus Christ His Son.

CHAPTER 10

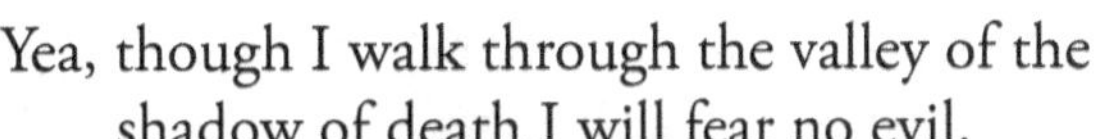

Yea, though I walk through the valley of the
shadow of death I will fear no evil.

—Psalm 23:4

WHEN WE WALK through life, we have a million questions about everything, especially questions that pertain to us and our lives. To walk is a physical action, a verb; to move, or walk can be figuratively speaking. The Bible answers or shows us how to walk in His word. We have already seen Psalm 23:4, "Yea, though I walk through the valley of the shadow of death, I will fear no evil." In the same verse, we see that it says, "for You are with me." What? God is with us? Have you ever heard that before? If you have not, let me tell you it is true. That's right, it's true, so get up off the ground and believe God's word, not Satan's lies. Satan never, never, never tells any truth.

To walk with God is sometimes easy, but many times, it's hard. It is hard because we are human, and we have sin in our lives from the minute we are born:

...They shall walk not faint. (Isaiah 40:31)

...And to walk humbly with your God. (Micah 6:8)

Then Jesus said to them 'A little while longer the
light is with you. Walk while you have the light,
lest darkness over take you; he who walks in dark-

ness does not know where he is going. While you have the light, believe in the light, that you may become sons of light. These things Jesus spoke, and departed, and was hidden from them. (John 12:35–36)

...Even so we also should walk in newness of life. (Romans 6:4)

What does this mean? It means that as a Christian, we should walk by faith not by sight (2 Corinthians 5:7), and we walk in the Spirit and not to fulfill the lust of the flesh (Galatians 5:16). Paul tells us in Ephesians 5:2 that "we walk in love, as Christ also has loved us and given Himself for us, an offering, a sacrifice to God for a sweet-smelling aroma." *Wow!* God said that when I walk with Him, I smell really good, and not nasty like the gooey scum at the bottom of the trash can, you know, when we are sinning.

All of us have questions for God. Don't we? Father, why? Father, when? Father, what? Father could? Father would? Many, many questions; some answered and some not, but all the questions to God. Many of these questions cause doubt, fear, even unbelief. Why do we have these questions? In Genesis 2:4, it states, "...This is the history of the heavens and the earth when they were created in the day that the Lord God Jehovah made the earth and the heavens." We humans question God. The media has brainwashed us and made us think that the Bible is just stories. There have been many intellectuals to challenge God's Word. These intellectuals have tried to dispel God's Word and concepts. However, the more they research, the closer to God they get. Before you know it, they come face-to-face with the living God, and they cannot deny Him. Just ask Lee Strobel, a national writer and journalist who set out to counter Christian belief and the Bible. That's when he wrote *The Case for Christ*, about how he came to know Christ is real.

"Jesus Christ is the same yesterday, today, and forever" (Hebrews 13:8). So we question God. We all do, all the time, especially in times of trouble or doubt. We think God has not heard our prayers. God is a covenant God. Jehovah means a covenant-keeping God. Jehovah Jireh, the Lord will provide. Jehovah Rapha, the God that heals. El Shaddai, all-sufficient One! So why, why, why are we asking God all the what, when, where, and why questions?

Jesus said, "Come to me, all you that are heavy laden, and I will you rest. Take My yoke upon you and learn from Me, for I am gentle and lowly in heart, and you will find rest for your souls. For My yoke is easy and My burden is light" (Matthew 11:28–30). The burdens of this world are painful. We ask why the pain is happening, what caused the pain, or is there a purpose for the pain?

> Why is my pain perpetual, and my wound incur-able, which refuses to heal? (Jeremiah 15:18)

> My heart is severely pained within me. And the terrors of death have fallen upon me. (Psalm 55:4)

> O my soul, my soul! I am pained in my heart. (Jeremiah 4:19)

God runs after us. He pursues us even when we are not behaving as His sons or daughters. Hebrews 12:11 tells us, "No chastening seems to be joyful for the present, but painful…" Psalm 116:3 states, "The pains of death surrounded me…and the pangs of sheol laid before me; I found trouble and sorrow."

Just when you think I am a goner. Just let me die! Come on! Now everyone of us has thought that at least once in our lifetime. Here is what we should know. Psalm 116:4 tells us, "Then I called upon the name of the Lord: O Lord, I implore You, deliver my soul." Acts 2:24 then says, "…Whom God raised up, having loosed the pains of death."

We cry out to God what is the purpose of the pain. King David, a man after God's own heart, cried out to God to deliver his soul from the pain. What is the purpose of the pain? Ecclesiastes 3:1 says, "To everything there is a season, a time for every purpose under heaven…" Jesus spoke in John 12:27, "…But for this purpose I came to this hour. Father glorify Your name."

I cry over everything. Do you cry? Some do and some are tough and wouldn't let anyone see them cry. God made me with eyes that pour tears. I cry when I am hurt, angry, happy, sad, or any other spectrum of emotions. That's how God made me. People think I am weak, but on the contrary, I am strong in Him who redeemed me. I could not have survived the circumstances of my past if Jesus had not been there. Did you know that God saves all of our tears? That's right. He, the Almighty King of the universe, takes time to save each and every tear we cry. Psalm 58:8 says, "You number my wanderings, put my tears into Your bottle…" God saves our tears, every tear, for any reason. Our tears are precious to God. Don't waste your tears for matters out of your control or waste your tears on people who have evil intentions.

Hebrews 12:14–17 speaks of Esau and how he sold his birthright for a morsel of bread, and later, he was rejected when he wanted to inherit his blessing. Verse 16–17 says:

> Lest there be any fornicator or profane person like Esau, who for one morsel of food sold his birthright. For you know that afterward, when he wanted to inherit his blessing, he was rejected, for he found no place for repentance, though he sought a diligently with tears.

Have you ever cried to get your way? Come on, be honest! I have! What do you think God thinks when we cry for the wrong reasons? He saves all our tears, but those tears must be a little sour!

Psalm 2:1 states, "Why do the nations rage, and the people plot a vain thing." First Corinthians 15:2 says "…By which you are saved, if you hold fast that word which I preached to you—unless you believed in vain." Vain, what does it mean? According to *Webster's Dictionary*, (a) vain is having or showing an excessively high opinion of one's appearance, abilities, or worth (conceited, narcissistic, self-loving, self-admiring), (b) producing no result, useless. Do we believe in vain? Because we are humans, we all have the sinful trait of vanity. Let's be honest; I am not pointing fingers, or I would have one on myself.

God's promise can be found in Revelation 21:4, "And God will wipe away every tear from their eyes; there shall be no more death, nor sorrow, nor crying. There shall be no more pain, for the former things have passed away." This is *good news*! We as Christians have the victory. We need to live like victors and not victims.

Fear is an unpleasant emotion caused by the belief that someone or something is dangerous, likely to cause pain, or a threat. I don't want to live in fear. To fear God is to have a sense of respect, awe, and submission to a deity. The Hebrew word *yirah* [yir—aw] means awesome, extremely, fearing, and reverence. "The Lord is my light and my salvation; whom shall, I fear?" (Psalm 27:1). Easy to say, right? Especially when at church or Bible study or Sunday school or even with our Christian friends. However, we are human with human feelings. I have a friend who told me, "We don't live in our feelings." That's easier said than done.

Feelings are an emotional state or reaction. So we fear God based on emotion? I mean fear God as in afraid of Him? In His word, we are to fear the Lord as in respect or revere. Psalm 111:10 states, "The fear of the Lord is the beginning of wisdom..." Okay, *wow*! When we fear through emotion, we allow ourselves to be open to Satan's influence. When we fear, we do not think clearly. I fear what people will think—pride. I fear what my children, husband, wife... are doing and what others think. Pride. Fear is an emotion closely related to pride; both are sin!

> The fear of man brings a snare, but whoever
> trusts in the Lord shall be safe. (Proverbs 29:25)

> ...be strong, do not fear! Behold, your God will
> come with vengeance, with recompense of God;
> He will come and save you. (Isaiah 35:4)

> For God has not given us a spirit of fear, but of power and of love and of sound mind. (2 Timothy 1:7)

> There is no fear in love, but perfect love casts out fear, because fear involves torment,…(1 John 4:18)

Love casts out fear. The Word is talking about God's love, Christ's love, not love of choice. God gives us free will and choice. Remember, God's love casts out fear. Fear is not of God or from God. Fear is from Satan. He wants to keep us a tangled mess, where we can't think. Remember King David said, "The fear of the Lord is the beginning of wisdom." This is reverence of God.

We, as Christians, want to trust God and know or be assured He is near. But do we really trust Him? We say we do, but does our heart trust him? In Isaiah 55, the prophet talks about an invitation to an abundant life, which includes trusting God. Our heavenly Father wants a covenant with us; in verse 3 it says, "Incline your ear to Me, hear, and your soul shall live; and I will make an everlasting covenant with you." How awesome is that? God wants a covenant with me, the girl who committed all the sins I have stated or not stated in this book. Wow!

God will make a covenant with you as well. You just have to ask. Isaiah said we must seek the Lord while He may be found (verse 6). In other words, while He is available; after all, if He pursues us, and we keep saying, "I'm okay, I'll seek You someday," He may give us our wish and let us stay in our sin and misdirection. But in verse 7 Isaiah says He will have mercy on us, which means He will forgive us if we ask. In verses 8 and 9 Isaiah says, "For My thoughts are not your thoughts, nor are your ways My ways…" God sees the whole picture; He knows all things. God speaks to us through His word.

Psalm 37:5 says, "Commit your way to the Lord, trust also in him," and in verse 37:7, "Rest in the Lord, and wait patiently for Him…" Proverbs 3:5 tells us, "Trust in the Lord with all your heart." Trust, commit, rest in Him the Lord God Almighty. Trust in Him with *all*, not part or a small piece, but with *all* your heart. If we trust in the Lord and commit our whole heart to Him, we can rest in His hand and salvation.

God's word says don't trust a friend; do not put confidence in a companion (Micah 7:5). God tells us our friends will turn on us in the right situation—children against parents, sons dishonor fathers, and daughters rise against mothers. Does this sound familiar? Children are committing murder on a daily basis on their elders. For what reason? To feed sin? When we have sin in our hearts, we do not trust in God our Father. If we don't respect our parents, grandparents, people who are over us like employers, bosses, supervisors, and the list goes on, then how can we respect God? With sin in our life, we rely only on ourselves. Mark 10:24 states, "…Jesus…said to them children how hard is it for those who trust in riches to enter heaven?"

Jesus was not saying it is bad to have riches. We all know people who have riches, but trust and serve the Lord. Jesus was saying you cannot trust in riches or anything of this earth and enter heaven. Trusting in Jesus is how we enter heaven. In Old Testament times, God came and went; that's why the writer of Isaiah 55 tells us to seek the Lord while He is near (verse 6). God speaks and guides us in His Word. So why do we have a trust issue with God? In the song by Tenth Avenue North "I Have This Hope," they sing, "I don't want to live in fear, I want to trust that you are near. Thrust Your grace can be seen in both triumph and tragedy." We pray for God's blessings, but are we willing to pray that God will use our brokenness for Christ? God's grace can be seen in our tragedies, our brokenness, our losses, and our disappointments. Psalm 55:17 tells us, "The sacrifices of God are a broken spirit, a broke and contrite (humble) heart. These O God, You will not despise."

Have you ever had your faith stretched until you almost broke like a stretched rubber band? I have. If God loves me, then why? Why? Why? Oh woe is me. Nobody loves me, everybody hates me, think I'll go eat worms.

Remember Job? Do you think his faith felt stretched and thin? He lost everything—all his children, all his animals, his house—and his friends turned on him. Even his wife said, "Curse God and die."

Job replied in 13:15, "Though He slay me, yet will I trust Him…" Though the Lord take my life, I will still trust Him! How many of us can say this?

In Mark 9, there is an account of Jesus healing a child. The father of the child wanted to believe but was still struggling with trusting God. The father said, "Lord I believe, help me in my unbelief" (verse 24).

God can take our sorrows, tragedies, joys, and successes and mold us and carve little pieces of sin off of us. We just have to trust Him, especially when we feel our faith being challenged. Remember God saves all our tears in His bottle because they are all precious to Him. Deuteronomy 31:6 states, "Be strong and of good courage, do not fear or be afraid of them; for the LORD your God, He is the One who goes with you… He will never leave you nor forsake you." God will never leave us, no matter where we are or what our sorrow or sin; God never leaves us behind.

God gives us reassurance in His word that He will never leave us: 1 Kings 8:57; 1 Chronicles 28:20; Psalm 37:28; Psalm 94:14; Isaiah 41:17; Isaiah 42:16; and Hebrews 13:5. God's word is true. He will never leave nor forsake us. These are just a few examples of His promise. No matter what we have done, no matter where we have been, He will forgive us if we confess with our mouth and just ask. Just ask; He is always there waiting for us to ask.

Never have we been closer to God than when we are down in the muck and mire. When we are so low and we *feel* forgotten. God is waiting for us to say, "Help me in my unbelief." Psalm 40:1–3 reminds us that God brings us up out of the miry pit, and He places our feet on a rock. He also puts a new song in our mouths. Our feet are placed on a rock; the rock is the foundation of our stability. An old hymn says, "On Christ, the solid Rock, I stand; All other ground is sinking sand. Jesus is our Rock, the corner Stone of the Temple." He calms the storms in our lives, just as He did when in Matthew 8:23–27 and Mark 4:35–41 Jesus walked out on the water with the disciples. With a raise of a hand, He calmed the storm, and He can calm the storms in us.

God reminds us of His promises and loves us beyond measure. God is our only hope. Psalm 37:4 says, "Delight yourself in the Lord, and He will give you the desires of your heart." The closer we are to God, the more our desires are the same as His desires. Matthew 6:33 tells us, "Seek first His kingdom, and all will be given unto you." This all that is spoken of all our needs like food, shelter, and healthcare; maybe not the new car or expensive vacation, but He will provide our needs.

Joel 2:25 states, "I will restore to you the years the locusts have eaten." God provides everything we need. He promises us He will never leave or forsake us. God is so close, and He wants your brokenness and my brokenness, your sin and my sin. John 3:16 says, "For God so loved the world, He gave His One and only Son, that whosoever believes in Him will not perish, but have everlasting life."

Never has God been closer than He is right now. He will take your pain, sorrows, and tears if you allow Christ into your heart and believe He is the Lord God our Savior. He will never leave us nor forsake us. God does not want us to waste our sorrows. He did not allow things into our lives to keep them and hoard them. All our hurts, sorrows, disappointments, and sins are used by God to help others see Christ through us.

In Isaiah 55:3b, it tells us, "I will make an everlasting covenant with you." A covenant is an unbroken promise. So a covenant with God can never be broken. We humans do break covenants with God and others every day. God calls us, God uses us, even the broken ones, the rebels, and the prodigals, for His glory. Once redeemed, always redeemed. An heir to the throne, a sister or brother to Christ. We have the same Holy Spirit living in us, and the same power as Christ.

CHAPTER 11

Therefore, we also, since we are surrounded by so
great a cloud of witnesses, let us lay aside every weight
and the sin which so easily ensnares us…

—Hebrews 12:1

MY PASTOR'S SERMON recently was mainly out of Genesis 20 and Hebrews 12:1 where it says, "…Let us lay aside every weight and the sin that ensnares us…" It said *the sin*, not our sins or your sins; it says *the sin* that entangles us. This *sin* is the one Satan always uses to weaken us. Each of us have at least one *sin*, that as a Christian, we are not proud of, and we may even hope no one finds out. We all know what *the sin* is in our life. It may not be there now because Christ redeemed us. Still, until we settle *the sin* by letting Satan know his seduction of *the sin* is fruitless, we will always be chained to *the sin*.

Christ redeems us, and He forgives us, but we are the ones who act as if we are still chained or imprisoned by *the sin*. My sin was lust. Lust of the flesh because I had a distorted view of love and affection. I have been overweight most of my life, and any attention toward me romantically I viewed as love. You have to know what *love* is. Love is a choice, an action, a verb. To love is a decision. Lust is *not* love. Lust is sexual action or thought outside of marriage, and it is sin. It was *the sin* that trapped me because I felt unworthy of being loved. I was teased and humiliated about my weight and how I would never have a boyfriend or a husband. A lie told by Satan! A lie that pierced my inner being. I began to believe it!

After all, I had never felt loved. I had hated my parents when I was young. I gave my mother permission to take her own life. How could anyone ever love me now? That's when it began. I loved a boy because he said he loved me. I ran away with him to many places for three months. Being fifteen, it was very hard to find and pay for the necessities of life. But I did love him. Our relationship was sinful in the eyes of God. When this relationship ended, I returned home, and every relationship I had with the opposite sex began and ended with sex, lust, and sin. My relationships were not healthy, and I can only praise God for His hand of protection. I was saved when I was twelve, so God's hand was on me, even if I did not know or acknowledge His protection or Him.

I lived my long years with heartache after heartache because I was a willing participant in *the sin*, and I couldn't understand why my relationships or marriages didn't work out. But God is faithful. Jesus left Judea for Galilee. He did not detour around Samaria like most travelers. Jesus told His disciples He needed to go through Samaria. John 4:5 says, "So, He came to a city of Samaria which is called Sycar (means drunker) near the plot of ground that Jacob gave to his son Joseph." Verse 6 continues, "Now Jacob's well was there… Jesus sat by the well…" Then verse 7, "A woman of Samaria came to draw water. Jesus said to her 'give me a drink…' And verse 9, "The woman asked, 'How is it You, being a Jew, ask a drink from me a Samaritan woman.'" Jews did not have dealings with Samaritans. Jesus told the woman she "had five husbands and one whom you have now is not your husband…" In other words, Jesus knew everything about her and all her sin. He introduced her to the life-giving water, where she would thirst no more. The Samaritan woman was seeking satisfaction, which was a void in her life until she met Jesus. We are all like the Samaritan woman; we were made with a void in us that only Jesus Christ can fill. We search through our sin never to be satisfied until Jesus fills the void.

Jesus sees who we are and what we have done in our past and what we will do in our future. He knows everything. When Jesus meets us, He meets us where we are. We don't have to get dressed up or cleaned up before we can meet Him. All we need to do is simply confess our sin(s) and accept Him as our Lord and Savior. We as humans try to complicate Jesus's acceptance. The woman at the well was so overwhelmed by her sins being forgiven that she left her waterpot at the well to go evangelize others. A waterpot was very valuable because a person had to gather their water daily.

So whether our sin is lust, jealousy, drunkenness, thievery, or murder, Christ Jesus will forgive us and receive us into His arms when we confess and ask for forgiveness. He will forgive us, and we would/could turn to the other direction and run from sin. We can change in an instant to follow Him.

For most of my life, I ran away from my circumstances searching for satisfaction, a way to fill the void in me and my life. The void was one I could not fill alone. I fell into more sin than I realized, and it started in my teens and followed me into adulthood. Once I truly understood, Psalm 139 opened my eyes as to who I am in God's eyes. He loves me, and He knew me before I was ever formed. He created me, and I am fearfully and wonderfully made (verse 14). You are fearfully and wonderfully made too! He created each of us unique just the way He wants us, so we can serve and worship Him.

No matter where we are in our sin, when we confess our sin with our mouths (Romans 10:9–13) and believe in our hearts, we will be saved. If we have been saved, we need to confess daily and ask forgiveness of our sins. Because we are human, we sin daily even if we have been saved or redeemed.

Remember the following verses:

> No man cometh unto the Father but by me.
> (John 14:6)

> For the wages of sin is death, but the gift of God
> is eternal life, through Jesus Christ our Lord.
> (John 14:6)

> For all have sinned and come short of the glory of
> God. (Romans 3:23)

For whosoever shall call upon the name of the Lord shall be saved. (Romans 10:13)

For God so loved ________________ [your name] that He gave His One and only Son, Jesus, and whosoever believeth in Him should not perish but have everlasting life. (John 3:16)

Where do you stand today? Jesus will meet you right where you are, just like He did me.

I am redeemed, a child of the King of glory, an heir to the throne of God. The *sin* that held me captive, the one that Satan used to tempt and seduce me, has been cast away by the blood of Jesus.

Psalm 34:18 says, "The Lord is close to the brokenhearted and saves those who are crushed in spirit."

CHAPTER 12

The Lord is my life and my salvation; Whom shall I fear?
The Lord is the strength of my life; Of whom shall I be afraid?
—Psalm 27:1

MY LIFE TODAY has taken on a different turn as I ponder my future and what it may hold. I have written a lot about my first love and loss, and I have also written about several failed relationships. I had other ungodly, sinful experiences with other male friends and acquaintances. None of these are worthy to be discussed here except to say I have been forgiven of these bad relationships, and God has redeemed me. I am not afraid to see or meet any of these men of my past because I have the strength that God empowered me with when He sent the Holy Spirit to live within me. I hope and pray that each of them has met and received Jesus into his heart and has lived a blessed and full life.

My biggest concern and worry today is my husband, who God placed in my life seventeen years ago (at this writing). He has a long-term illness and receives chemo treatments every four weeks. I worry that I will experience his passing. Then I will be alone again. This time, God has given me a passion for His word to sustain me. God has truly blessed me with a full life. Although I have made some stupid decisions in my past, He knew every little detail of my life, and He created me anyway.

Psalm 139 speaks about how God knew me before I was formed, and He wrote my name in His book. I know in my head that fear does not come from God, but I do fear that one day God will take him home because of his cancer. Our prayers will be answered that God would heal my husband. It will be the perfect healing, to be taken home to heaven. I am just selfish that I came to understand God and His work in my life late in my life. What if I had been only with my first love? I don't know where I would be. I do know that I would not have met any of my other relationships or husbands because I would have been self-exiled from my family. At fifteen, what kind of life could I have forged? I don't turn back time, and I don't wish to remove any of my circumstances because God has used each one to mold me and make me who I am in Christ Jesus. Isaiah 41:10 states, "Fear not, for I am with you; be not dismayed for I am your God; I will strengthen you."

I attended a ladies' function at church recently, and the speaker asked us to think about the first time we had heard the word *worthy* as it applied to our lives. The first time the word worthy was used in my life I was about forty years old. Wow! I had gone all my life and I had no clue as to how God saw me or thought of me. He created me. He knew me. He wanted me. He loved me. I had no clue!

Like I have said, when I received counseling during my early forties, I was introduced to Psalm 139, where it explains what God thought of me and you. He said, "You are fearfully and wonderfully made…" As I reflect on my life and all the past mistakes I made, as an adult I want to shake the younger me and scream, "*What were you thinking?*" I can't go back and change anything nor would I want to.

God uses every circumstance in our lives to form our character and personality, so someday we will use those mistakes and sins for His glory and purpose. God was always working in my life, even when I wasn't. God knows everything about us. He knew I would run, that I would give over my purity to someone outside of marriage. We committed to each other, but can a couple, both fifteen years old, make a sound decision about life and commitments? I said yes, I could, he said he could, and we made a covenant to each other and God. Both of us were in survival mode, both coming from difficult lives. He had been given up for adoption at four to protect him from abuse. He had run away from his foster or adoptive parents to seek out his biological mother. I ran because I was on an emotional roller coaster that was like a runaway train without breaks. I was burning like a wildfire that could not be contained. We were in love and running from life.

Back to this word *worthy*, I have never heard this word or understood this. My counselor told me that the way we think of ourselves is 80 percent based on lies. What? Lies that others tell us and lies we tell ourselves. In James, He teaches us that God has given each of us the gift of *self*. This gift is in the divine image of God, but turned in upon itself, self becomes the source of temptation, the evidence of sin, and the obstacle to holiness (James 1:14). James reminds us we are not self-sufficient like we think we are. We are searching and seeking for something to fill the void that God created within us. Only He can fill that void. Only He can satisfy our needs and wants. Only He accepts us and meets us where we are. He created us, and He loves us. He will never leave or forsake us. When we accept Christ in our lives, we are worthy in His eyes.

God is so good. God used the love in my life to protect me while He was allowing me to make ungodly decisions. God continues to work on us and mold us to His perfection, even when we are not walking with Him. My biggest concern during that time in my life was getting caught. There were no cell phones, no technology, no computers, no instant information system. I chose to come home, reluctantly. I lived in captivity until I was forced into marriage due to pregnancy a few months after I graduated from high school. I was released from the strict environment to my husband. I was told that I could not come home again, my key was taken, and I was on my own.

My life continued down the road that was broken with sin, sorrow, and unworthiness, until one day when I was introduced to Psalm 139. I discovered how God really saw me in my entirety, and He chose to make me anyway. Through Christ, He forgives me, He loves me, and I am worthy in His eyes. God never stops working on us. He loves us so much that He never leaves us. When we *feel* like we have no one that cares for us, God is waiting for us to cry out to Him for help from our sin. John 8:32 says, "You will know the truth, and the truth will set you free."

Just as God honored Samson's faith in spite of his sin (Joshua 2:4–5), God honors our faith in spite of our sin. This is a relief to me as my sin was great. Just as Samson's sin was lust of pagan women, my sin was lust to provide acceptance and worth to my feelings. I felt unworthy and unwanted. The opposite sex (after my first love) provided a false sense of love, affection, and acceptance. A false sense from who? Satan! Satan is the producer of false teaching and lies, the tempter to destroy us and our testimony. Praise God! He still has a plan for my life, a plan of victory and fulfillment through Him.

I have written and rewritten my story many times. I have added to it each time, and the more I add, the more I ache for the loss of God's blessings due to my decisions and taking roads off His path for my life. My prayers are that you, the reader, will not find justification for sin but forgiveness and salvation through Christ's forgiveness of sins. He will forgive and redeem each and every one that confesses with their mouth that Jesus Christ is Lord. Blessings and peace to you.

EPILOGUE

Though He slay me, yet I will still trust Him…

—Job 13:15

GOD ALLOWED SATAN to test Job, even though Job had not done anything wrong against God. Job was considered righteous and just in the eyes of God. My story was not like Job's; however, God allowed testing and wandering in my life that my character would be honed and carved in the likeness of His Son, Jesus. Just as the potter pounds the clay and molds it into a worthy vessel, God has been carving and molding me all these years that I might resemble Him someday. It has been two years since I last wrote my testimony, and I thought you, the reader, might want an update from my last chapter.

My husband, Mike, continued his chemotherapy for about a year. He developed fluid around his heart, and this caused great distress. He was taken to the hospital and placed on a ventilator in a controlled coma like state, until his heart could heal. I was able to stay with him 24-7 in his room. As I watched him and prayed for him for five days and nights, I talked to God continuously. Christian friends and prayer warriors from several churches laid hands and prayed over him. On the fifth day, he was slowly awakened from his sleep, and the ventilator was removed. He spent five more days adjusting to breathing on his own and preparing to return home.

One month later, in May 2019, Mike was returned to the hospital for the same problem, fluid around his heart. This time we caught the symptoms in time, and there was no need for a ventilator.

After a few days, he had surgery on the pericardium around his heart, where a 3X3 inch window was cut to avoid future fluid retention. The following June 2019, he was back at the hospital again for dehydration and an infection that had to be cleaned out. In September 2019, Mike had his right kidney removed. The lab results revealed no live cancer cells. He has been considered cancer free. The doctors have expressed amazement at his diagnosis, treatment process, and his prognosis. The doctors who first began treatment of him in August 2018 did not expect him to live until September 2019 and the removal of the kidney. I expected nothing less because my God and King had revealed to Mike that he was to go home and be with Mary.

Today, July 2021, I wanted to update everyone on the progress that our lives have taken. God has been so good to us. Mike has been able to keep his job throughout all of his illnesses and hospital stays (six times in one year). I have not been able to acquire a full-time teaching position; however, I substitute teach regularly during the school year. God has provided for us and has stretched our budget in ways we could never have on our own. The year of COVID-19 has come and gone. The world is slowly moving back to a new normal. Last month, June 2021, Mike and I had our eighteenth anniversary, and this is the first summer he has not been sick since our move to the mountains. Life is good because God is good.

My final thought is that I would wrong you, the reader, if I did not lead you to know Christ Jesus as our Lord and Savior. "For the wages of sin is death but the gift of God is eternal life, through Jesus Christ our Lord" (Romans 6:23). "For all have sinned and come short of the glory of God" (Romans 3:23). But in Romans 10:13, "For whosoever shall call upon the name of the Lord, shall be saved." "For God so loved the world that He gave His One and only Son, that whosoever believeth in Him should not perish but have everlasting life" (John 3:16). "If you confess with your mouth Jesus is Lord and believe in your heart that God raised Him from the dead, you shall be saved…" (Romans 10:9). "Come unto me, all you that labor and are heavy laden, and I will give you rest" (Matthew 11:28–30). "No man cometh to the Father but by Me" (John 14:6). "There is now no condemnation for those who are in Christ Jesus" (Romans 8:1).

In the song, "We Have Heard the Joyful Sound," the first and last verses praise God for our salvation.

We have heard the joyful sound.

> Jesus saves! Jesus saves!
> Spread the tidings all around:
> Jesus saves! Jesus saves!
> Bear the news to every land,
> Climb the steeps and cross the waves;
> Onward!—'tis our Lord's command;
> Jesus saves! Jesus saves!
> Give the winds a mighty voice,
> Jesus saves, Jesus saves;
> Let the nations now rejoice.
> Jesus saves, Jesus saves;
> Shout salvation full and free,
> Highest hills and deepest caves,
> This our song of victory,
> Jesus saves, Jesus saves.

I will leave you with this thought: even when I chose badly, God was still watching over me. He does not want us to waste our sorrows. He wants us to share our lives and life circumstances to His glory. God is still on the throne, and Jesus is King.

ABOUT THE AUTHOR

MARY'S STORY IS one of hardship, disappointments, and poor decisions. Yet her story has a reflective approach that reveals God's plan and protection over her life. Her desire is that everyone would come to know Christ and that her story would plant a seed of hope, forgiveness, and healing to those who read it.

Mary lives in the North Georgia mountains with her husband and three dogs. She has four children and four grandchildren. Mary found Christ in her youth but developed her relationship with Christ as an adult. She has been active in several churches leading Bible studies, teaching Sunday school, working with youth and elementary children, and missions. She enjoys writing and reflecting on God's word and the relationship that is built with Him in the process.

www.ingramcontent.com/pod-product-compliance
Lightning Source LLC
Chambersburg PA
CBHW030810170726
47995CB00011B/379